A Trail Guide to the Maah Daah Hey Trail, Theodore Roosevelt National Park, and the Dakota Prairie Grasslands

A Trail Guide
to the
Maah Daah Hey Trail,
Theodore Roosevelt
National Park, and the
Dakota Prairie Grasslands

HIRAM ROGERS

Johnson Books
BOULDER

Published by Johnson Books, a division of Big Earth Publishing, 3005 Center Green Drive, Suite 220, Boulder, Colorado 80301. www.johnsonbooks.com
E-mail: books@bigearthpublishing.com

Cover Design: Constance Bollen, cbgraphics
Text Design and Composition: Michel Reynolds
9 8 7 6 5 4 3 2 1

Library of Congress Cataloging-in-Publication Data
Rogers, Hiram
    A trail guide to the Maah Daah Hey Trail, Theodore Roosevelt National Park, and the Dakota Prairie Grasslands / Hiram Rogers.

      p. cm
    Includes bibliographical references.
    ISBN 1-55566-358-3
    1. Hiking—North Dakota—Guidebooks. 2. Hiking—North Dakota—Maah Daah Hey Trail—Guidebooks. 3. Trails—North Dakota—Maah Daah Hey Trail—Guidebooks. 4. Hiking—North Dakota—Theodore Roosevelt National Park—Guidebooks. 5. Trails—North Dakota—Theodore Roosevelt National Park—Guidebooks. 6. North Dakota—Guidebooks. 7. Maah Daah Hey Trail (N.D.)—Guidebooks 8. Theodore Roosevelt National Park (N.D.)—Guidebooks I. Title.

    GV199.42.N69R64 2006
    796.5109784—dc22

                                            2006017856

Contents

Tables and Maps

Acknowledgments

T HIS GUIDE would not have been possible without the help of many people. The following people generously answered questions and reviewed manuscripts for trails in their areas of responsibility: Curt Glasoe, Dakota Prairie Grasslands; Bruce Kaye, Theodore Roosevelt National Park; Jane Muggli, Theodore Roosevelt Nature and History Association; Terrence O'Halloran, Knife River Indian Villages National Historic Site; Phil Sjursen, Dakota Prairie Grasslands; and Russ Walsh, Dakota Prairie Grasslands.

My wife, Jean, shares my fondness for this remarkable area. She read much of the manuscript, scouted many of the new trails, and endured many evenings filled with my muttering, scrawling, and thrashing through trail maps. Without her love, humor, and patience, this project would never have been completed.

MAP A

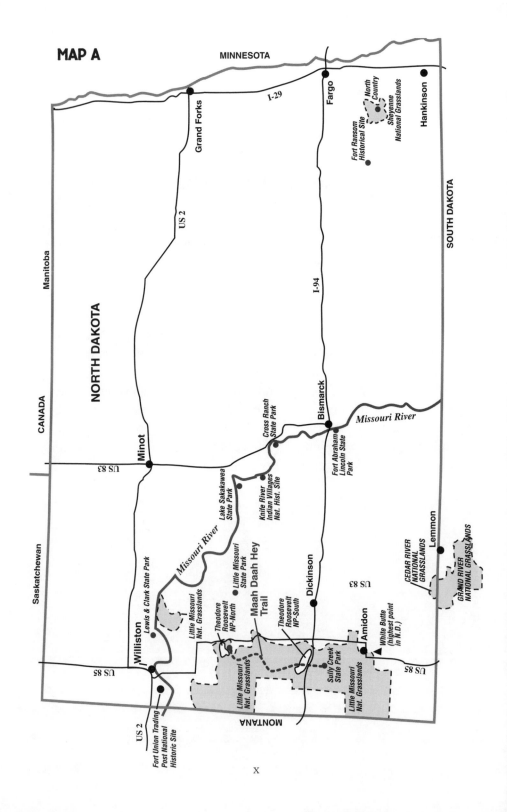

Introduction

THE BADLANDS of western North Dakota are a beautiful and unique area. The exceptional potential of this wonderful recreation area is just starting to be developed and discovered by pioneer hikers, mountain bikers, and horse riders. This guide focuses on hiking, mountain biking, and horseback trips in two main areas: Theodore Roosevelt National Park (TRNP) and the surrounding Dakota Prairie Grasslands (DPG), along with the 96-mile-long Maah Daah Hey (MDH) Trail.

Some of the material in this book previously appeared in *Exploring the Black Hills and Badlands: A Guide for Hikers, Cross-country Skiers, and Mountain Bikers*. When that book was first published in 1993, the only significant trail systems in western North Dakota were in Theodore Roosevelt National Park, so it made sense to cover North Dakota in a single chapter of a larger book. Since that time, the Maah Daah Hey Trail—connecting the North and South units of the Theodore Roosevelt National Park—has been completed. The Maah Daah Hey Trail has been a tremendous success with mountain bikers, horse riders, and hikers, and it has spawned a second wave of trail building in the Dakota Prairie Grasslands. Between the national park, DPG, and state parks there are nearly 300 miles of trails in this region. In addition, there are nearly another 100 miles of trails in the Sheyenne and Grand River districts of the DPG, the Knife River Indian Villages National Historic Site, and various North Dakota state parks. With increased trail use in Theodore Roosevelt, the completion of the Maah

Daah Hey Trail, and the development of other trail systems in the region, the time has come for a trail guide dedicated to this unique area.

A dedicated guidebook to the area means that trail descriptions can be more complete and more detailed. In Theodore Roosevelt National Park, all the major trail loops are now described. I have added descriptions of the Upper Paddock Creek–Upper Talkington Loop in the South Unit, and the Buckhorn Trail in the North Unit. Most importantly, this guide contains the first detailed trail description for all of the 96-mile Maah Daah Hey Trail. The Maah Daah Hey Trail offers a unique combination of scenery, solitude, and excitement that has made it an instant favorite of anyone who has had the fortune to travel on it.

The success and popularity of the Maah Daah Hey Trail has led to the development of a series of side trails in the surrounding grasslands. The first and most important of these is the Buffalo Gap Trail, which was built to offer mountain bikers a route around the wilderness area in the South Unit of Theodore Roosevelt National Park. The Dakota Prairie Grasslands has used the Maah Daah Hey Trail as the backbone of a system of trails unparalleled in the national grasslands system. Fourteen other trails form short loops and link the Maah Daah Hey Trail to various campgrounds and to the Ice Caves.

To complete the coverage of the trails in the Dakota Prairie Grasslands I've expanded this guide to include a 28-mile section of the newly rebuilt North Country National Scenic Trail in the Sheyenne Ranger District. Two other DPG trails, the Blacktail Trail near Shadehill Reservoir and the Hankinson Hills Trail in the southeast corner of the state also are described here for the first time.

A few other trails outside the national park and national grasslands are included as well. Public access to North Dakota's highpoint at White Butte remains open, thanks to the generosity of understanding local landowners. The rise in popularity of "highpointing," climbing the high points of all fifty states, ensures that White Butte will remain a popular destination. The extensive trail system at Little Missouri State Park is included. This trail system has grown to 47 miles since my first visit in 1992, and the park has become very popular with horse riders. Along the Missouri River between Garrison Dam and Bismarck lie several scenic trail systems. In addition to the western end of the North Country National Scenic Trail at Lake Sakakawea State Park, trails at Knife River Indian Villages National Historic Site and Cross Ranch State Park are described here for the first time. To complete coverage of the North Country National Scenic Trail, an active section of it in Fort Ransom State Park is described.

One of the difficulties of writing trail guides is anticipating changes that might take place while the guide is in print. The Maah Daah Hey Trail is already undergoing a series of improvements, primarily to lessen grades and reduce the potential for erosion. Additional connecting trails may be built, but the most significant changes could be the proposed extension 40 miles south to Burning Coal Vein Campground and the development of a designated mountain bike bypass route around the North Unit of Theodore Roosevelt National Park. The Dakota Prairie Grasslands may also continue to build new trails away from the Maah Daah Hey Trail in other areas of the grasslands. If you plan to go exploring in the DPG, check in with them for the latest information.

Table One – Trip Planner

		DIST	RATING	FAMILY	MB	HORSE	BP
TRNP	Jones Creek–Lower Paddock Creek Trails Loop	11.0	M	P	N	Y	Y
TRNP	Upper Paddock Creek–Upper Talkington Loop	15.4	D	N	N	Y	Y
TRNP	Petrified Forest Loop	15.0	D	P	N	Y	Y
TRNP	Caprock Coulee Nature Trail	4.3	M	Y	N	N	N
TRNP	Buckhorn Trail	11.4	M	N	N	Y	Y
TRNP	Achenbach Trail Loop	17.6	D	N	N	Y	Y
MDH	Sully Creek Campground to Wannagan Camp	17.1	M	N	P	Y	Y
MDH	Wannagan Camp to Elkhorn Camp	21.4	M	N	Y	Y	Y
MDH	Elkhorn Camp to Magpie Camp	19.7	M	N	Y	Y	Y
MDH	Magpie Camp to Bennett Camp	21.8	M	N	Y	Y	Y
MDH	Bennett Camp to CCC Campground	16.0	M	N	P	Y	Y
DPG	Buffalo Gap Trail	18.9	M	N	Y	Y	Y
DPG	Ice Caves Trail	1.5	E	Y	Y	Y	N
DPG	Cottonwood Trail	7.1	M	Y	Y	Y	Y
DPG	Bennett Trail	3.1	E	Y	Y	Y	Y
DPG	Long X Trail	5.8	M	N	Y	Y	N
DPG	Summit Trail	3.8	M	Y	Y	Y	N
DPG	North Country National Scenic Trail/Sheyenne Section	28.2	M	P	Y	Y	Y
DPG	Blacktail Trail	6.7	E	N	Y	Y	Y
DPG	Hankinson Hills Trail	7.8	M	N	Y	Y	Y
ND	White Butte, Highest Point in North Dakota	3.0	E	Y	N	N	N
ND	Travois Indian Trails Loop, Little Missouri State Park	4.0	E	Y	N	Y	Y
ND	Knife River Indian Villages National Historic Site	12.9	M	Y	N	N	N
ND	Cross Ranch State Park and Nature Preserve	15.9	M	Y	N	N	N

Key: E = easy, M = moderate, D = difficult, P = parts, MB = Mountain Bike, BP = overnight backpacking

Using This Guide

THE TRIPS described in this guide range from short, self-guided interpretive trails, such as Caprock Coulee in Theodore Roosevelt National Park, to multiday expeditions, such as a trip along the entire Maah Daah Hey Trail. While each trip may not be suitable for everyone, there is a broad range of trip ideas ranging from outings for families with children, to suggestions for experienced backpackers looking for multiday excitement. Trips are included for hikers, mountain bike riders, and horse riders. The trips, their length, difficulty, and allowed uses are summarized in Table 1.

The book is divided into four main sections. The first covers the trails in Theodore Roosevelt National Park. The next two cover the Maah Daah Hey Trail and the rest of the trails on the Dakota Prairie Grasslands. The final section covers other trails outside of the grasslands and Theodore Roosevelt National Park, including White Butte, Little Missouri State Park, Knife River Indian Villages National Historic Site, and Cross Ranch State Park.

The first three chapters begin with an overview of the natural and cultural history of that area. General background information on the features of the area follows along with a summary of that area's rules and regulations. Next come the trip descriptions, which are given in two levels of detail. The most popular, or most deserving, trips are described in detail, while some of the other trails and routes are briefly described.

Those described as *trails* follow officially mapped and maintained trails. Those described as *routes* (White Butte, MDH's North Unit Bypass, and the return leg of the Petrified Forest Loop along the Little Missouri River) follow unmaintained and unsigned routes of my own creation.

Each detailed trip profile begins with a brief description that also indicates which user groups are allowed and how difficult the trip is. This heading, along with the information in Table 1, is designed to help visitors quickly select the trip that is right for them. The allowed uses of a trail vary according to the land management agency. Most importantly for users of this guide, note that mountain bikes are not allowed on the trails in Theodore Roosevelt National Park.

Trail difficulty can be very tough to gauge. Distance, elevation changes, and roughness of footing are the most important factors. But the weather on any particular day can make a bike trail slippery or leave a hiker cold and wet. Since there is such a range between the strongest hikers seeking challenging trips and casual hikers seeking shorter diversions, these ratings can only be a rough guide. When planning your trip, keep in mind both the rating and distance. The terrain on a 20-mile stretch of flat trail may be easy, but it doesn't take long for all those miles to add up. If you're not sure of your abilities, be conservative. The longer trips will always be there to challenge you on later visits. I can tell you from hard-earned experience that it is better to have some energy left when you get back to the car, than to struggle through a long afternoon simply hoping to reach the end of the trail.

- "**General Location**" lets you easily find a trail from the nearest town using either a highway map or your favorite mapping software.
- "**Trip Highlights**" help readers select trails that will most interest them. Here you'll find out if a particular trail is known for wildlife watching, has outstanding vistas, or is ideal for seekers of solitude.
- "**Access**" gives detailed driving directions on how to reach each trailhead from a nearby town or major highway. For one-way trips, directions to both trailheads are given.
- "**Distance**" is given in miles for each trip, and often for optional variations. These distances may vary somewhat from those listed else-

where. In a few cases distances have been measured more accurately, and in others I've chosen a slightly different version of a popular trip.

Finally, there is a list of useful trail maps. The maps contained in this guide are based on the official maps from the parks and grasslands units described here. A few changes have been made as a result of my own experiences in the field. Most of the areas described in this guide are covered by the National Geographic Trails Illustrated map of Theodore Roosevelt National Park, which also covers all of the current Maah Daah Hey and Buffalo Gap trails. Rather than try to replicate all the mapping information in the Trails Illustrated map we have presented generalized trail maps, and refer those wanting more detail and a topographic base to the Trails Illustrated map.

Two other sets of maps will also prove useful to the outdoors lover. The U.S. Geological Survey (USGS) maps for both the South and North Units of Theodore Roosevelt National Park are still in print at a scale more detailed than the Trails Illustrated map. The 7.5-minute USGS 1:24,000 quadrangles for western North Dakota were recently updated and now show the Maah Daah Hey Trail. The Medora Ranger District also sells a generalized map of the Maah Daah Hey Trail and a map of the Dakota Prairie Grasslands. The relevant USGS maps along with any other important park maps are listed.

Keep in mind that there are several errors in the route of the Maah Daah Hey Trail on the new USGS 7.5-minute quads, and a few errors on the first edition of the Trails Illustrated map as well. Where there are discrepancies between the USGS and Trails Illustrated maps for the Maah Daah Hey (for example, north of the Cottonwood–Maah Daah Hey intersection at mile point 75 on the MDH) I have always found the Trails Illustrated map to be correct.

The level of detail contained in trip descriptions corresponds to the difficulty of finding your way. Descriptions for well-marked trails are brief, while those of obscure trails or unmaintained routes are very detailed. It is a good idea to check with the appropriate management agency (see Appendix B) before starting on an unfamiliar trail and to check your map each time you stop when on an unfamiliar trail or route. To help mountain bikers in selecting their trips, the surface for each trip is described as a trail, two-track dirt road, maintained dirt road, or gravel road.

Global positioning system (GPS) units have become popular instruments for both techies and outdoors lovers. GPS units use readings from a satellite network to triangulate the position of the unit, often to within 50 feet. I've used a GPS to map some of the trails in this guide. The Trails Illustrated map has both latitude and longitude and UTM coordinates using a NAD 27 Datum. If you depend on GPS for your navigation, remember that it can be impossible to get GPS readings, especially in canyon bottoms, and that good, old-fashioned map and compass use may be needed.

The road network in the Dakota Prairie Grasslands is evolving. There may be many more roads than are shown on U.S. Geological Survey, Trails Illustrated, or DPG maps. Avoid the temptation to navigate solely by watching road intersections. I have simplified the DPG road classification system by naming all roads by number with an agency name prefix. These roads are generally permanent, are signed, and have numbers such as DPG Road 808. These roads may also have county road numbers and names.

Trail systems throughout the region are being expanded and improved. Be aware that a trail guide cannot remain current forever, and that the conditions of trail markers can deteriorate over time. If you find an error in a trail description or other notable feature, or discover a relocation in one of the trails, let us know about it so we can include the change in the next edition of this book. Write me in care of the publisher at: Johnson Books, 3005 Center Green Drive, Suite 220, Boulder, Colorado 80301 or via their website at www.johnsonbooks.com.

Enjoying the Outdoors

THE TRAILS described in this guide can be used for hiking, mountain biking, and horseback riding. These trails can be used nearly year-round. Though winter is usually too severe to enjoy outdoor recreation, a few days may be warm and calm enough to enjoy some sheltered hiking. A few trails described here are also groomed for cross-country skiing. Cool temperatures, without lingering snow, can make spring hiking ideal. In summer, escape from the heat by mountain biking, hiking in the woods along a cool river, or by leaving the work to a willing horse. In fall, dry soil and mild weather combine to allow superb hiking and riding anywhere in the region.

Day hikes in western North Dakota require only a little advance planning before you set out. You need to know the length of the route, and whether the trip requires a car shuttle. In summer, your main worries are water, plus sun and wind protection. Essential items to carry include food, water, a first aid kit, sunscreen, lip balm, and a hat for shade. Few trailheads provide drinking water, and you should never drink untreated water. Snakes, bison, and other wildlife can pose hazards for hikers. Do not disturb any wildlife you encounter. Be aware that poison ivy grows in many moist areas.

Backpacking skills for the North Dakota badlands can be quite different from those used in other areas. Badlands backpackers are exposed to an all-day onslaught of sun and wind. The major factor in trip planning is that some areas have no water, and you must provide all of yours. The weight and bulk of a large water supply can be a major burden on a long trip, so some parties in Theodore Roosevelt National Park may elect to hike in a short distance and set up a base camp. Another alternative, especially for those hiking long distances on the Maah Daah Hey Trail, is to cache water along your route. Badlands backpackers don't suffer the physical toil of hauling heavy loads up high mountains, but they are exposed to extremes of weather in an unforgiving wilderness terrain. However, the views here are always 360 degrees, nature's bounty is readily apparent, and many of these areas are true wilderness seen by few other visitors.

The Dakota Prairie Grasslands is paradise for **mountain bike** riders. The Maah Daah Hey and the other trails around it are scenic, challenging, and relatively uncrowded. Mountain bike riders should also prepare for their trips with an eye on the weather. A gentle rain, or even a heavy dew, can turn a normally easy trail into an unridable obstacle course of sticky, slippery gumbo. Be sure to bring repair tools, a tire pump, and patch kits. Don't plan on being able to call for a ride if things go wrong. Riders should also wear a helmet and gloves for those inevitable crashes.

Horseback riding is one of the most popular activities on the Maah Daah Hey Trail and on the trails in Theodore Roosevelt National Park. Riders should keep in mind that conditions in both the park and grasslands are primitive. Water, potable or not, is difficult to find away from the major rivers. Trails can be extremely slick when wet or even just damp. Riding on wet trails can severely erode them, so confine your trips to dry conditions. Horses can be hired from concessionaires at the South Unit of Theodore Roosevelt National Park and at Little Missouri State Park. All riding areas described here require certified weed-free feed for horses.

Family trips are listed in Table 1. These trips are short and easy enough to accommodate younger hikers, and also have the high-impact features and end-of-trail rewards that will hold the interest of youngsters. If a trail is too long for families, but a shorter piece is suitable, it is marked with a "P" in Table 1.

All-terrain vehicle (ATV) use is becoming more widespread. The Forest Service nationwide has identified unregulated off-road vehicle use as one of the most significant threats facing our national forests. Many parts of the Dakota Prairie Grasslands, and most of the trails described here, are closed to vehicle use. The Forest Service has just begun a major shift in the way that it manages transportation. In general, vehicles have been allowed in areas unless specifically prohibited. The new policy will allow ATV use only where specifically designated. The shift from this "open, unless indicated" to "closed, unless indicated" management style will likely take several years to implement. Expect the Forest Service to step up its efforts nationwide to prevent cross-country ATV use.

Recommended Trips

T HE TRIPS listed below are generally my personal favorites, although some were chosen with the help of some other experts. Most have at least one or two special features such as tremendous views, wilderness solitude, or wildlife watching to recommend them. If you don't have a lot of time to explore the area, these are the trips to take.

A subjective list from the easiest (1) to most difficult (5).
BEST HIKES FOR KIDS
1. Ridgeline Nature Trail, TRNP, South Unit
2. Coal Vein Trail, TRNP, South Unit
3. Little Mo Nature Trail, TRNP, North Unit
4. Caprock Coulee Nature Trail, TRNP, North Unit
5. White Butte

BEST DAY HIKES
1. White Butte
2. Painted Canyon, TRNP, South Unit
3. Caprock Coulee Nature Trail, TRNP, North Unit
4. Jones Creek, TRNP, South Unit
5. Buckhorn, TRNP, North Unit

BEST BACKPACK TRIPS

1. Buckhorn, TRNP, North Unit
2. Petrified Forest Loop, TRNP, South Unit
3. Achenbach Loop, TRNP, North Unit
4. Sully Creek to Wannagan Camp, Maah Daah Hey Trail
5. Bennett Camp to CCC Campground, Maah Daah Hey Trail

BEST MOUNTAIN BIKE RIDES

1. Bennett–Cottonwood–Maah Daah Hey Loop
2. Buffalo Gap Trail, DPG
3. Maah Daah Hey Trail, Wannagan Camp to Elkhorn Camp
4. Maah Daah Hey Trail, Magpie Camp to Bennett Camp
5. Maah Daah Hey Trail, Elkhorn Camp to Magpie Camp

BEST ROAD BIKE RIDES

1. South Unit Scenic Loop Drive
2. North Unit Scenic Drive

BEST RIDES ON HORSES

1. Long X, DPG
2. Jones Creek–Lower Paddock Creek, TRNP, South Unit
3. Little Missouri State Park
4. Painted Canyon, TRNP, South Unit
5. Buckhorn, TRNP, North Unit

Theodore Roosevelt
National Park

T HEODORE ROOSEVELT is the national park that best exemplifies
the spirit of the American West. Here one can imagine this rugged
country as it was in the late 1800s, during the days of Roosevelt's cattle
ranching. The landscape remains unchanged: humankind's influence on
this unforgiving land has been modest. Just as during Roosevelt's tenure,
only a few isolated ranches dot the landscape, and cattle ranching
remains the primary occupation. The Little Missouri badlands may now
be even richer in wildlife than they were then. Roosevelt arrived near
the peak of the cattle boom, when bison and other game species had
been overhunted. Between the natural recovery of some populations
and the reintroduction of others, the region's wildlife may now be more
prolific.

Theodore Roosevelt came to the Dakotas in 1883, when western
North Dakota was becoming known for ranching and hunting. Few
bison remained when Roosevelt first arrived for a hunt; but he fell in
love with the country and soon returned to try ranching. This was the
era of open range, when cattle grazed without fences. Unfortunately for
ranchers, this cattle boom was short-lived. The harsh winter of
1886–1887 killed large numbers of stock, and the subsequent summers
were much drier.

This short period in the Dakotas profoundly influenced Theodore
Roosevelt. Roosevelt's Maltese Cross Ranch was located south of
Medora, but he preferred life on his more isolated Elkhorn Ranch.
Ranching fit well with his philosophy of a vigorous life. His writings are

filled with an appreciation for the quiet simplicity of ranch life, and for the beauty of the natural world. He witnessed the near extinction of bison and emerged from the experience as a powerful force in American conservation. The beauty and solitude found today in this national park is a fitting tribute to the president who most strongly shaped our conservation ethic and national park system.

The movement to establish a national park to honor the former president began soon after Roosevelt's death in 1917. The area was first designated a national wildlife refuge in 1946, and it became a national memorial park in 1947. As the management focus of the area shifted from historic preservation to broader stewardship of natural resources, the area was made Theodore Roosevelt National Park in 1978.

Theodore Roosevelt National Park is divided into three separate units—separated by 40 miles of private land and Dakota Prairie Grasslands. The South Unit, located adjacent to Interstate 94 (I-94) near Medora, covers 46,000 acres and receives the most visitors. Forty miles north, off U.S. 85 near Watford City, the North Unit covers 24,000 acres. Between the two units, set snuggly against the Little Missouri River is the 218-acre Elkhorn Ranch Unit, nearly as isolated now as when it served as Roosevelt's primary residence. The three areas are tied together by the region's lifeline, the waters of the Little Missouri River. In addition to protection as a national park, three parcels also were designated as the Theodore Roosevelt Wilderness in 1978. In the South Unit, 10,500 acres, including most of the area west of the Little Missouri, is designated wilderness. In the North Unit, 19,400 acres—in two areas split by the Scenic Drive—are also designated wilderness. Wilderness designation gives these lands the highest degree of protection possible, by prohibiting activities such as use of mechanized vehicles or the building of roads or other permanent structures.

Entry Fees and Visitor Centers

A seven-day entry pass to the park is $5 per person, up to $10 per vehicle. A variety of other passes are available through the National Park Service. Most visitors will first stop by one of the park's visitor centers. The South Unit is on mountain time, while the North Unit is on central time. The Painted Canyon Visitor Center is at Exit 32 on I-94. It is open from 8 A.M. to 6 P.M. mountain time from mid-June through Labor Day, and from 8:30 A.M. to 4:30 P.M. mountain time from April through mid-June and from Labor Day through October. The Medora Visitor Center in the South Unit is open from 8 A.M. to 6 P.M. mid-June to Labor Day, and until 8 P.M. on weekends. It is closed Thanksgiving Day, Christmas, and New Year's Day, but is open 8 A.M. to 4:30 P.M. mountain time the rest of the year. Tours of Roosevelt's restored and relocated Maltese Cross cabin are conducted daily in summer. Though most visitors arrive in summer, the swing seasons of spring and fall offer milder weather for those seeking to explore the trails.

The North Unit Visitor Center is open 9 A.M. to 5:30 P.M. central daylight time Memorial Day through September. It also is closed Thanksgiving Day, Christmas, and New Year's Day. The rest of the year it is open as staffing permits.

Camping and Picnic Areas

In the South Unit, the Cottonwood Campground, 5.6 miles from Medora on the Scenic Loop Drive, is open year-round. The right loop has larger pull-through sites, and the left loop has smaller sites. There are no utility hookups. Of the 78 sites, 12 are walk-in tent sites. Campsites are available on a first-come, first-served basis. In 2005, sites were $10 per night. Reservations are accepted only for the group camp (6 to 20 people). The campground has flush toilets (in summer only) and a pay phone, but does not have showers. There are no dump facilities for trailers at the campground. The nearest dump facilities are in Medora. A full list of rules and a map are available at the check-in station and any visitor center. Livestock, including horses, are not allowed in the campground. Pets must be kept on leash, a commonsense rule in an area that may be visited by bison, wild turkey, and other wildlife. The campground is open year-round with well water and latrines available in winter.

The Juniper Campground, located at mile point 4.6 on the North Unit Scenic Drive, is also open year-round. There are 50 sites in two loops. Campsites are available on a first-come, first-served basis. In

2005 sites were $10 per night. Reservations are accepted only for the group camp (6 to 60 people). The campground has flush toilets (in summer) and a pay phone, but does not have showers. Juniper has dump facilities for trailers. A full list of rules and a map are available at the check-in station and any visitor center. Livestock, including horses, are not allowed in the campground. Pets must be kept on leash, a reasonable rule for an area where game trails across the Little Missouri River may bring bison into your camp during breakfast or dinner. Juniper Campground can also serve as the trailhead for the Achenbach, Buckhorn, and Little Missouri (Little Mo) Nature trails. In winter there are latrines only and the nearest water source is the North Unit Visitor Center.

The Roundup Group Horse Camp is located in the South Unit about two miles north of the end of the Scenic Loop Drive. The camp is open to groups of 6–20, usually from May 1 to November 1. Starting in 2006 reservations will be selected from a mail-in lottery process, rather than the old first-come, first-served telephone process. For 2006, the first day for accepting mail or fax requests was March 6. Fees are $2 per person and $1 per horse per night with a $20 minimum. Facilities include vault toilets, drinking water, a pavilion, and picnic area, plus corrals, hitch rails, and water tanks. Certified weed-free horse feed is required, and horses must follow designated trails. A full list of rules and a map are available at the check-in station and any visitor center. Other information on horse boarding around the park can be obtained from the visitor centers.

A wide variety of commercial campgrounds are located in communities around the park. Picnic areas are located next to the Cottonwood and Juniper campgrounds, at the Painted Canyon Visitor Center, and in Medora.

Hiking

No permits are needed for day hiking trips in the park, although it is always wise to ask at a visitor center for the latest trail conditions. If you plan to cross the Little Missouri River, make sure you check river levels before beginning your trip. Remember also that wet weather can make much of the backcountry impassable, especially areas where the soil contains a bentonite clay, locally called gumbo. This devilish substance is firm and chalky gray when dry. But when wet it has the unique ability to be both sticky and slippery at the same time. It can be too slick to walk on safely, but at the same time it can cling in huge heavy masses to boots, bike tires, and horse hooves.

Remember that all plants, animals, and historic artifacts in the park are protected, and must be left undisturbed for the enjoyment of other visitors. Be especially careful to give wildlife a wide berth. Bison in particular can be unpredictable; lone bulls can be especially grumpy. Rolling in dirt or raising their tails (this display can mean "charge" or "discharge") are signs of agitation, and a good warning for hikers to flee. More than likely you'll encounter ticks, and both poison ivy and rattlesnakes are found in the park.

One of the unusual things hikers notice about the trails at Theodore Roosevelt are the huge wooden posts used to mark them. These monsters are usually six inches square, and five feet high. They are buried deeply in the ground, but nonetheless are often toppled by the ever-present bison. The bison, which use the trails more than people do, have nothing against trail markers. But they do love to scratch on the posts, particularly those dotting the grasslands where nature has left them few natural options. Presumably, scratching is the most intense in the spring when winter coats need to be shed in advance of summer's blast of heat. But year-round you'll find tufts of brown fur clinging to slivers of the marking posts. How many posts mark your trail will depend on the balance between the longing of bison for good scratching posts, and the perseverance of the park rangers in replacing them. Since some visitors found the park's distinctive "Ted Head" trail markers confusing, TRNP plans to replace the signs that had an iconic rendering of Theodore Roosevelt's portrait with a simpler generic hiker symbol.

Trail maintenance in the park varies with the resources the park is allocated each year. Bison are efficient, if unintentional trail builders. If you have strayed onto a game trail, retrace your path back to a marked trail. However, a good map, and attention to it, is enough to keep most hikers on course in the open terrain. Cross-country travel on foot is allowed anywhere in the park, and route finding for those with maps and map reading skills is straightforward.

Spring and fall are the best times to visit the Little Missouri badlands. The change in seasons moderates the temperature extremes characteristic of the northern plains. Many visitors will find the heat and absence of shade in midsummer uncomfortable. Try to do most of your activity in the early morning or late evening. As always, keep an eye on the weather. It never takes long to go from dusty to downpour.

Biking

There are no trails open to mountain bikes in Theodore Roosevelt National Park. Bikes must stay on paved roads, a restriction that leaves the scenic drives as the only realistic biking options in either park unit. The South Unit Scenic Drive is a 35.7-mile round trip from Medora and the North Unit Scenic Drive is a 27.4-mile roundtrip. However, there are numerous mountain biking options in the surrounding Dakota Prairie Grasslands. For information on mountain biking on the Maah Daah Hey Trail and its surrounding trail network, see the following chapter on the DPG.

Horse Riding

A trip on horseback through Theodore Roosevelt National Park gives the same view from the saddle that Roosevelt himself had during his tenure in North Dakota. The easiest introduction to horseback riding in the park is to visit Peaceful Valley Ranch. The ranch offers trail rides daily during the summer season. The basic trail ride lasts 90 minutes, leaves several times a day, and includes interpretive information about the park. For experienced riders, longer rides are available by scheduling in advance.

Those looking to organize their own trip can board horses at Peaceful Valley, the Roundup Group Horse Camp, or at a number of private areas outside the park (check at the visitor center for a current list). You should make arrangements for horse boarding before arriving at the park.

Horses are allowed on all the backcountry trails and are allowed to go cross-country away from the developed areas of the park. Horses are not allowed on the developed nature trails, on roads, in campgrounds, or in picnic areas. Two popular riding trails from the Roundup Group Horse

Camp are the Mike Auney Trail that leads west to the Petrified Forest Loop Trail, and the Roundup Camp Trail that leads east to the Jones Creek Trail. Another popular area is the maze of trails along the Little Missouri bottomland in the vicinity of Peaceful Valley Ranch.

Horse groups spending the night in the backcountry are subject to the backcountry camping regulations discussed below. Horse riders on day trips are also subject to the same rules as other park visitors. The park has an overnight limit of eight horses and eight riders per group. Remember that grazing in the park is prohibited, and certified weed-free feed is required for your horses. Be especially careful not to harass wildlife. The park prohibits horses from coming within 300 yards of bison.

Backcountry Camping

Anyone staying overnight in the backcountry of TRNP must obtain a backcountry camping permit from either the Medora or North Unit visitor center. The permits are free, although park entry fees still apply. Please check out at the visitor center, or return your permit, after your trip. There are no designated campsites or restrictions on the number of parties in particular areas. Campsites must be at least one-quarter mile from roads or trailheads and at least 200 feet from water sources. Party size limits are ten people, or eight people plus eight horses.

Backpackers and horse parties are subject to the same guidelines as those on day trips. In addition, the park requires all campers to practice Leave No Trace camping techniques. A full list of regulations is printed on the park backcountry trail map. Some important regulations include a ban on open fires in the backcountry, a ban on pets, the need for hikers to yield right-of-way to horses, and the need to carry out all trash (burying trash is prohibited). Dispose of human waste in a cat hole that is at least 200 feet from any campsite or water source.

Depending on your route, locations along the Little Missouri River or close to flowing wells will offer the best campsites. Due to the lack of drinking water in the backcountry you will need to plan where to camp in advance of your trip to have access to water and the ability to treat it. Occasionally it is possible to get water from larger side creeks such as Knutson Creek, but these creeks only flow during the wettest seasons

MAP B: Theodore Roosevelt National Park - South Unit

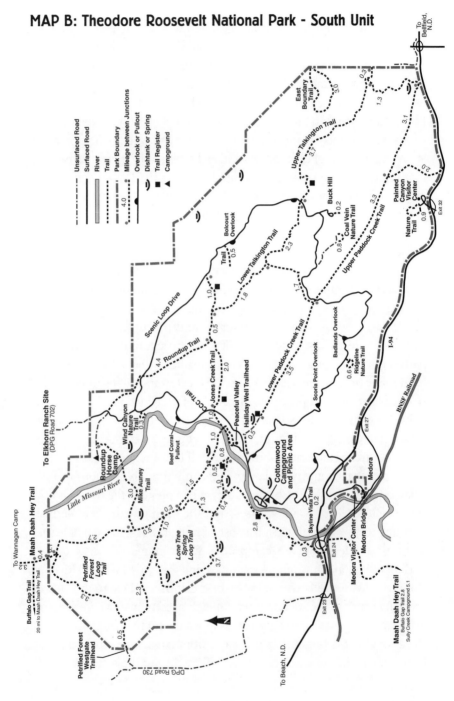

Unsurfaced Road
Surfaced Road
River
Trail
Park Boundary
Mileage between Junctions
4.0
Overlook or Pullout
Dishtank or Spring
Trail Register
Campground

or immediately after storms. Wells and springs found in the backcountry have nonpotable water suitable for wildlife and livestock only.

Jones Creek–Lower Paddock Creek Trails Loop, South Unit

Description: A rugged circuit through the center of the South Unit for hikers or horses.

General Location: Three miles north of Medora, North Dakota.

Highlight: The wildlife watching includes bison and prairie dogs.

Access: From the South Unit Medora Visitor Center, drive north on the paved Scenic Loop Drive for 8.4 miles to the parking area at the Jones Creek Trailhead. If your group has more than one vehicle, leave one at the Halliday Well Trailhead to avoid 1.5 miles of hiking along park roads.

Distance: The loop is 11.0 miles around.

Maps: Theodore Roosevelt National Park Backcountry Guide, USGS Theodore Roosevelt National Park South Unit 1:24,000 special topographic map, Trails Illustrated Theodore Roosevelt National Park (#259), and Map B, *page 22*.

One of the most popular trips in Theodore Roosevelt National Park is a loop that connects the trails along Jones and Paddock creeks. This loop can be hiked in one long day, or combined with the Upper Paddock Creek and Talkington trails to make an overnight trip. The lower loop follows quiet creek bottoms through country much rougher than other trails in the South Unit.

Begin by hiking east on the *Jones Creek Trail*, crossing the main fork of Jones Creek twice. As the trail winds along the creek bottom through green ash and grasses, notice how clusters of juniper are found only on the shaded and moister north-facing slopes. Near 2.0 miles the *Roundup Camp Trail* leads left 4.4 miles to the Roundup Group Horse Camp. At

Hikers near Jones Creek

the next junction at 2.5 miles, the Jones Creek Trail continues left to reach the Scenic Loop Drive in 1.0 mile. However, our route turns south to follow the *Lower Talkington Trail* over a butte that marks the divide between Jones and Paddock creeks to reach another junction at 4.3 miles. From here we leave the Lower Talkington Trail, which will reach the Scenic Loop Drive in 2.3 miles, and follow a connector trail, which branches south from the Talkington Trail.

Follow the connector trail south down a small tributary. The last one-half mile of the connector trail is adjacent to the park loop road. Along the way, pass areas where erosion of sandstone in the Bullion Creek formation has produced steep sand dunes. Reach Paddock Creek, and a small turnout from the road, which marks the *Lower Paddock Creek Trail* at 6.0 miles.

Follow the Lower Paddock Creek Trail downstream and west to reach the Halliday Well Trailhead at 9.5 miles. Notice how the meanders in Paddock Creek are tighter and more closely spaced than the meanders in the Little Missouri River. The rate of water flow in a stream, the gradient of the stream, and other properties of a watershed are related to the size of the stream. Streams cut meanders as a means to dissipate the potential energy of water. Subsidiary streams, such as Paddock Creek, have high potential energy, which is spent on cutting more frequent meanders, while main streams, such as the Little Missouri River, have less potential energy and therefore more gentle meanders. The high level of erosion in subsidiary streams means that the bed of the stream is rougher and the flow turbulent. Despite appearances, water in a turbulent, subsidiary stream flows at a slower rate than water in a larger, smooth flowing river.

The Lower Paddock Creek Trail passes through a remarkably large prairie dog town where bison often graze. The town fills the entire valley floor as you approach the Scenic Loop Drive. If you were unable to leave a car at the Halliday Well Trailhead, you must walk 0.5 mile northwest along a dirt road, then 1.0 mile north along the Scenic Loop Drive to the Jones Creek Trailhead. You may walk along the road, or follow a maze of trails created by the park's horse concessionaire on the west side of the road. Experienced hikers can also take a shortcut north from the prairie dog town, and head cross-country back to the Jones Creek Trailhead.

Upper Paddock Creek–Upper Talkington Loop, South Unit

Description: A loop through remote backcountry with spectacular wildlife viewing.
General Location: Seven miles northeast of Medora, North Dakota.
Highlight: The wildlife watching includes wild horses.
Access: Exit Interstate 94 at Medora and proceed to the South Unit visitor center in Medora. From the visitor center follow the paved Scenic Loop Drive for 14 miles to a pullout where Paddock Creek and its namesake trails cross the Scenic Loop Drive.

Bison at Cottonwood Campground

Distance: A 15.4-mile loop. A shorter loop from Buck Hill is 10.5 miles.
Maps: Theodore Roosevelt National Park Backcountry Guide, USGS
Theodore Roosevelt National Park South Unit 1:24,000 special topographic map, Trails Illustrated Theodore Roosevelt National Park
(#259), and Map B, *page 22.*

The Upper Talkington and Upper Paddock Creek trails give hikers and
horse riders the chance to combine some of the park's most rugged
scenery with primetime wildlife watching. This loop can be done as a
long day trip or overnight backpack trip.

The loop begins by following the north side of the wide valley of
Paddock Creek. This valley is one of the favorite places for the park's wild
horses. If you spot the herd, look for the lead stallion working to keep
the group together. TRNP's feral horses descend from domesticated animals that escaped into the wild. Early in the history of the park, attempts
were made to remove horses. However, in 1970 the park decided to
manage them as part of the historical setting, consistent with conditions
during Roosevelt's time. There are now around 90 horses roaming free in
the South Unit. Deer and grouse are also common in this area.

After pulling away from the creek, reach a marked intersection with
the Painted Canyon Trail at 3.3 miles, just after crossing a major side
creek coming in from the north. The trail next reaches Southeast Corner
Spring at 6.4 miles. If you choose to use water from the spring for
drinking, remember that it must be treated.

From Southeast Corner Spring climb briefly to the grasslands, then
turn north on the connection to Talkington Trail. At 7.7 miles, intersect
the Upper Talkington Trail. From this point a spur leads east 0.3 mile to
the park boundary. The main route leads west and quickly leaves the
level grasslands at a point that may not be well marked. After a short
descent, reach a huge prairie dog town.

Beyond the prairie dog town, the trail is well marked. As the trail winds
to the northwest look for cannonball formations in some eroding rock
outcrops. At 11.4 miles cross the Scenic Loop Drive and start on the
Lower Talkington Trail. The trail follows a small creek valley, then climbs
to reach the junction with the connector trail to Jones Creek at 13.7 miles.

Turn left on the connector to reach the Paddock Trailhead at 15.4 miles.

For those planning to stay overnight on this loop, finding water will be a problem. Southeast Corner Spring is your only source, and this water should be treated before drinking. The spring area itself is not an ideal campsite. As the name implies it is very close to the park boundary and Interstate 94, not the remote and quiet campsite that this loop deserves.

Those experienced in off-trail travel, and looking for a shorter loop, can make a 10.5-mile loop by starting at Buck Hill. From Buck Hill simply hike south toward Paddock Creek and intersect the trail west of the junction with the Painted Canyon Trail. Then, follow the loop around to the Scenic Loop Drive. Near the end of the trip, instead of crossing the Scenic Loop Drive onto the Lower Talkington Trail, walk back to Buck Hill via the Scenic Loop Drive and Buck Hill Road.

Petrified Forest Loop, South Unit

Description: An overnight hike into the South Unit, which includes an off-trail hiking option along the Little Missouri River.

General Location: Three miles north of Medora, North Dakota.

Highlight: Petrified trees and wildlife watching in a wilderness setting.

Access: Exit Interstate 94 at Medora and proceed to the South Unit Visitor Center in Medora. From the visitor center follow the paved Scenic Loop Drive for 6.8 miles north to Peaceful Valley Ranch. Parking is available at the saddle horse concession. If the Little Missouri River is too high to ford, try the one-half mile West Entrance Spur Trail from the park's west boundary. Ask for a copy of the map and directions to the trailhead from the South Unit Visitor Center. Or, access the loop via the Maah Daah Hey Trail where it enters the park at Exit 24 on I-94.

Distance: The off-trail loop is about 12.0 miles long. The Petrified Forest Loop Trail is a 15.0-mile loop.

Maps: Theodore Roosevelt National Park Backcountry Guide, USGS Theodore Roosevelt National Park South Unit 1:24,000 special topographic map, Trails Illustrated Theodore Roosevelt National Park (#259), and Map B, *page 22.*

Backcountry hiking is the best way to experience Theodore Roosevelt National Park and the Little Missouri badlands. The park has a beautiful, well-developed trail system that is perfect for easy weekend backpacking trips. A loop on the west side of the South Unit combines two areas of special interest, the Petrified Forest Plateau and the bottomlands along the Little Missouri River, and offers an option for exploring off trail.

From Peaceful Valley, negotiate a maze of paths leading down to the Little Missouri River. In high water, crossing the river may be the most difficult part of the trip. Check current conditions before attempting a crossing. Once across, follow the Petrified Forest Loop Trail 0.8 mile up the riverside bluffs onto Big Plateau. Be aware that the trails around Peaceful Valley can change as the horse concessionaire at Peaceful Valley Ranch finds easier routes to access the plateaus.

Fording the Little Missouri River

Big Plateau is covered by a large prairie dog town, and the plateau also attracts mule deer, coyotes, and bison. Beyond Big Plateau, climb another bluff onto Petrified Forest Plateau. Along the base of this short climb, the trail crosses a distinct geologic horizon, which contains many of the fossil trees that give their name to the plateau. Several weathered fossil stumps are visible from the trail. Remember that the National Park Service prohibits collecting fossil wood in order to preserve the specimens that remain. At the top of the climb, reach a junction with the *Lone Tree Spring Loop Trail* and the *Maah Daah Hey Trail* at 2.3 miles. The two trails join until a split is reached at 2.6 miles at the start of the loop.

On the Petrified Forest Trail, stay right at the split where the Maah Daah Hey Trail also goes right. At about 3.1 miles the Mike Auney Trail leads right 3.0 miles to the Roundup Group Horse Camp. Enjoy another mile of almost perfectly level walking before the plateau narrows to form a gentle ridge, which extends toward the north boundary of the park.

If you want to stay on trails from this point, continue along a narrow ridge to the north boundary at 5.8 miles. Here the Maah Daah Hey Trail branches right to leave the park and enter the rugged Wannagan Creek badlands. The loop branches left to return to the Petrified Forest Plateau. Descend to reach an impressive "grove" of fossil wood before reaching a junction with the West Entrance Spur Trail at 9.1 miles. In one more mile visit another wood locality during a brief descent off the plateau. Intersect the *Lone Tree Spring Loop Trail* at 11.4 miles, and close the loop at 12.4 miles. Retrace your route to reach the trailhead at 15.0 miles.

If you want to complete an off-trail loop via the Little Missouri River, leave the Petrified Forest Trail near the north boundary, and hike northeast down a series of bluffs to the river bottom. A fine cluster of fossilized stumps sits nearby on a small bench just below the level of the trail. An easy descent route follows an abandoned jeep track along the nose of a small ridge before dropping into a small draw. Two groves of cottonwoods between the north boundary and VA Well offer campsites.

A riverside camp has the advantage of water, otherwise unavailable in the backcountry. The wells found scattered throughout the park are

Little Missouri Bottomlands

water sources for wildlife, and do not produce potable water, so treatment is necessary. An added bonus is that the river, which seemed so cold when you waded across in the morning, may by afternoon be warm enough for swimming. The bluffs on either side of the river are perfect for wildlife watching or photography.

On the second day, follow the river upstream for five miles back to Peaceful Valley, crossing the Mike Auney Trail. Bluffs along the river can be climbed or bypassed by wading in the river. Pass through another huge prairie dog town at Beef Corral Bottom. Beyond the prairie dog town, cross the river once more to avoid bushwhacking along the narrow strip between the river and the paved park road. End your hike at the parking area at Peaceful Valley.

The rocks in Theodore Roosevelt National Park were originally deposited as sediments during the Paleocene epoch. Rocks of the Bullion Creek (also called Tongue River) and Sentinel Butte formations, which are both part of the Fort Union Group, are found. These sediments were deposited by the rivers and streams that drained the ancestral Rocky Mountains to the west. At this distance from the mountains the streams carried clay, silt, and sand, which are now the soft siltstone and sandstone beds of the Fort Union Group. As the ancient Rocky Mountains began to rise, a chain of volcanoes became active in what is now Montana and Wyoming. Huge eruptions of these volcanoes sent ash as far east as the Dakotas. These ash deposits are found in the park as beds of bentonite, the clay mineral commonly called gumbo when wet. Bentonite has the remarkable ability to absorb five times its weight in water. Even more remarkable is how difficult bentonite is to walk on, or drive over, when wet. Gumbo is extremely sticky and slippery at the same time. There is no cure, only prevention; it is best to stay out of the badlands after a recent rain.

Recent paleontological excavations by the North Dakota Geological Survey in the Sentinel Butte and Bullion Creek formations have discovered fossils of a 55-million-year-old crocodile-like reptile called champosaurus. To learn more about the dig, and the park's rich fossil history, visit the paleontology exhibit at the Medora Visitor Center.

Petrified wood is common throughout Theodore Roosevelt National Park. The rapid rate of Paleocene sedimentation accounts for the formation of fossil wood. In the Paleocene climate much of the landscape was covered by thick forests and swamps. After rapid changes in stream channels, or volcanic eruptions, many trees were buried before they decayed. Following further burial, groundwater began to circulate through the sediments. Silica that was dissolved from the ash beds was then redeposited in the wood as groundwater saturated the buried trees. Eventually silica replaced and coated much of the woody plant tissues to create petrified wood. In well-preserved specimens, growth rings and other features are still visible. The most common type of petrified wood in the park is preserved tree stumps.

Caprock Coulee Nature Trail, North Unit

Description: The first three-quarter mile of this loop is a self-guided nature trail.
General Location: Thirteen miles south of Watford City, North Dakota.
Highlight: Spectacular geology and sweeping vistas.
Access: From U.S. 85, drive 6.5 miles west on the paved Scenic Drive to Caprock Coulee Nature Trail Pullout on the north side of the road.
Distance: The loop is 4.3 miles.
Maps: Theodore Roosevelt National Park Backcountry Guide, USGS Theodore Roosevelt National Park North Unit 1:24,000 special topographic map, Trails Illustrated Theodore Roosevelt National Park (#259), and Map C, *page 34.*

If you have time for only one hike in the North Unit of Theodore Roosevelt National Park, it should be the Caprock Coulee Nature Trail. The first three-quarter mile of this trail is a self-guided introduction to the geology and botany of the badlands and prairie. Beyond the self-guided portion lies some of the best ridge line walking found in the park. This trail is closed to horses.

Follow the numbered posts north from the trailhead along Caprock Coulee. At 0.1 mile a connector trail splits right to connect to the *Buckhorn Trail*. At the end of the self-guided trail, turn west, then south, to climb through a grove of juniper and green ash. Western wheatgrass is the dominant grass in these groves. The trail turns west again at the top of a narrow ridge. Follow the ridge west as it widens into open prairie before reaching the paved Scenic Drive at 2.7 miles.

Follow the Scenic Drive south to Riverbend Overlook at 2.9 miles, where a side trail leads south to a stone shelter. The trail stays on the roadside and crosses the heads of two small coulees. Then turn right off of the road onto the crest of a ridge leading east. Keep left at a junction with the

MAP C: Theodore Roosevelt National Park - North Unit

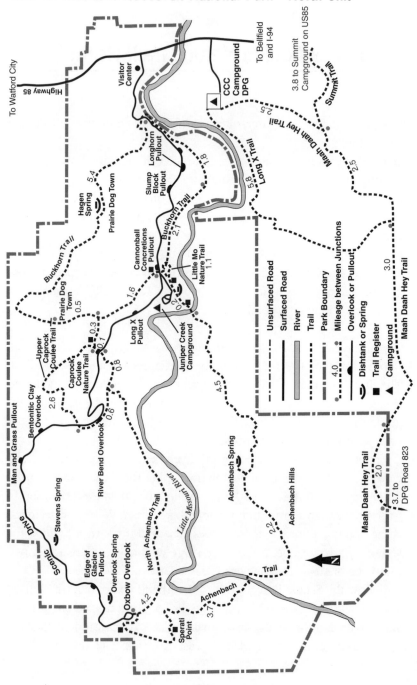

Riverbend Overlook

North Achenbach Trail at 3.5 miles and continue east. Cross two small saddles offering spectacular views over the Little Missouri River, before turning north off of the ridge. Descend steadily to the trailhead at 4.3 miles.

The diversity of the Caprock Coulee Nature Trail makes it an ideal introduction to Theodore Roosevelt National Park. The trail crosses most of the park's major habitats: sharp-edged coulees, juniper groves, narrow badlands ridges, and open prairie. The views are superb, particularly on the south side where the trail overlooks the Little Missouri River. Coyotes, mule deer, and rabbits find the trail easygoing, and you may also see tracks from one of the park's rare bobcats.

The display of geologic features along the trail is also impressive. On the self-guided portion, you'll learn how water cuts the soft bedrock and creates badlands. You will see examples of lignite seams, bentonite beds, landslides, slump blocks, and caprocks.

Theodore Roosevelt National Park personnel, along with assistance from the North Dakota Fish and Game Department and researchers from Montana State University, began an effort to introduce bighorn sheep into the North Unit in 1996. Native Audubon bighorns became extinct in the early 1900s from hunting pressure and loss of habitat. An effort by the North Dakota Fish and Game Department to transplant California bighorn sheep into the Little Missouri badlands began outside of the park in 1956 and eventually included the South Unit. The earlier effort resulted in a stable herd of around 250 sheep. However, the historic sheep range in the North Unit of Theodore Roosevelt was unoccupied until 19 California bighorns were released into the park in 1996.

Eight lambs were born the first year and seven more were born in 1997. The band mingles with other groups living outside the park. But for the most part, 15–20 of the newcomers remain in the park near the areas that researchers expected. Theodore Roosevelt National Park has a long history of successful wildlife reintroductions, which includes bison in 1956 and elk in 1985.

There is no water on the Caprock Coulee Nature Trail, and you'll probably appreciate a refreshing drink after being exposed to North Dakota's special combination of sun and wind. The Scenic Drive is open as far as the Caprock Coulee Nature Trailhead in winter.

Buckhorn Trail, North Unit

Description: A perfect introduction to the diversity of habitats found within the North Unit.

General Location: Thirteen miles south of Watford City, North Dakota.

Highlight: The wildlife watching includes bison and longhorn cattle.

Access: From U.S. 85, drive 4.9 miles west on the paved Scenic Drive to the Cannonball Concretions Parking area, which is located directly opposite the entrance to the Juniper Campground.

Distance: An 11.4-mile loop open to hikers and horses. With a car shuttle you can skip the last four miles that closely parallel the Scenic Drive.

Maps: Theodore Roosevelt National Park Backcountry Guide, USGS

Theodore Roosevelt National Park North Unit 1:24,000 special topographic map, Trails Illustrated Theodore Roosevelt National Park (#259), and Map C, *page 34.*

The Buckhorn Trail is an ideal introduction to the diversity of habitats found in the North Unit of Theodore Roosevelt National Park. Along the way hikers will visit immense prairie dog towns, pass herds of bison, and may even spot part of the park's small herd of Texas longhorn cattle. The terrain along the loop includes open prairie, high tablelands, and narrow canyons carved into steep slopes.

From the parking area, start north along the base of a small badlands cliff. At 1.1 miles a short unmarked side trail leads left to the Scenic Drive at Long X Trail Pullout. Past this junction the Buckhorn Trail becomes hard to follow. Keep heading north, and avoid any path that crosses Squaw Creek or veers toward the road, to stay on the main trail.

At 1.6 miles, reach a junction with a side trail that leads left for 0.3 mile to the *Caprock Coulee Nature Trail.* Keep right at the junction and you will cross a small draw at 2.1 miles and enter a large prairie dog town. At the north end of the prairie dog town, older maps show an old trail leading west, but this route has been reclaimed by the prairie and is now invisible. The Squaw Creek valley north of the town is favored by bison, so be careful not to surprise these giants. Bison are the largest mammal in North America. Bulls can reach a height of six feet at the shoulder and weigh up to 2,600 pounds. The smaller females can still reach an impressive five feet six inches and 1,100 pounds. The slaughter of the great bison herds in the late 1800s is a shameful story we all know well. By the time these magnificent animals were protected in the late 1890s only a few hundred remained in the wild. But bison have proved to be resilient, and once again they thrive in their native habitat. In 1956, 29 bison were brought to the South Unit, and this herd did well enough to seed the North Unit herd by 1962. Now the park manages both herds to keep around 450 bison in the South Unit and another 150 in the North Unit.

Leave the valley of Squaw Creek where the faint remnant of an earlier trail continues north to the park boundary. Make a sharp turn to the

Hiker on the Buckhorn Trail

southeast and keep a careful lookout for trail posts protruding from the deep sagebrush. But sage isn't the only plant in this valley; chokecherry, textile onion, dandelion, and coreopsis can also be found. When the valley splits, the trail follows the right side of the left fork through layers of concretions, bentonite, scoria, and petrified wood. Climb through a grove of juniper to reach an open plateau with some of the park's farthest views.

Near the end of the plateau pass another prairie dog town on the right of the trail. The descent from the plateau is perhaps even more scenic than the views from the top of it. You'll make two crossings of an unnamed creek that is favored by mule deer before climbing along the west side of the creek. At 7.5 miles, reach the Scenic Drive just to the west of a bridge over the creek.

Cross the road and follow a narrow strip between the road and a fence along the edge of the bluff high above the Little Missouri River. You'll soon reach the spacious bottomland where the river rounds a wide meander. Watch here for large herds of bison and the park's few remaining longhorn cattle. It is more important to give these animals a wide berth than to follow the scattered signposts that mark the trail. At 9.3 miles, reach a gravel road that leads to the park's bison management corral.

As you continue west, note the effects that fire has on sagebrush. New bushes spring from the charred remains of those consumed in a controlled burn. The park has an active prescribed burning program with a goal to treat 1,000 to 2,000 acres yearly. As you climb over a small saddle, notice a small pond on the left. The final section of trail involves crossing the road to the Juniper Campground's waste facility and two crossings of the *Little Mo Nature Trail*. After the second crossing of the nature trail, follow a two-track dirt road back to the trailhead at 11.4 miles.

Achenbach Trail Loop, North Unit

Description: A multiday wilderness loop for hikers and horses.
General Location: Fourteen miles south of Watford City, North Dakota.
Highlight: Wilderness solitude along the Little Missouri River.
Access: From U.S. 85, drive 4.9 miles west on the paved Scenic Drive. Turn south onto the road to Juniper Campground. The Achenbach Trail starts across the river from the campground.
Distance: Use parts of the Caprock Coulee and Buckhorn trails to form a 17.6-mile loop.
Maps: Theodore Roosevelt National Park Backcountry Guide, USGS Theodore Roosevelt National Park North Unit 1:24,000 special topographic map, Trails Illustrated Theodore Roosevelt National Park (#259), and Map C, *page 34.*

The Achenbach Trail explores some of the roughest terrain found in Theodore Roosevelt National Park. In the park's North Unit, relief is greater and the terrain more rugged than in the South Unit. Except for a narrow corridor around the park's Scenic Drive, most of the North Unit is designated wilderness. Through the heart of this country is a loop long enough for a two- or three-day trip. Before attempting to cross the Little Missouri River, check with the park staff on current conditions.

From Juniper Campground, hike 0.2 mile southwest to the Little Missouri River. Ford the river, and then cross the floodplain, before climbing through a mixture of badlands and juniper groves. Once onto the prairie above the river, follow the trail west, and then south to a point near the park boundary. Continue west on a north-facing slope to reach a junction with an old two-track road that leads southeast to the park boundary. Then enter the Achenbach Hills and reach a junction with a well-traveled trail leading north to Achenbach Spring, a source of nonpotable water, at 4.7 miles.

Continue across the Achenbach Hills through open prairie. Descend gradually to reach the Little Missouri River at 6.9 miles. Take special care to follow the trail along the river bottom and across the river. Hike about one mile north along the west side of the river before climbing steadily up to Sperati Point. Once out of the valley and onto the prairie, continue north to a junction with an old dirt road. Then hike north through the prairie for one-half mile before turning east to reach Oxbow Overlook and the end of the Scenic Drive, at 10.6 miles.

From the overlook, descend steadily back down to the river bottom. The North Achenbach Trail follows the north edge of the river bottom to the crossing of Appel Creek. From Appel Creek climb gradually east, then steadily north to reach a junction with the *Caprock Coulee Nature Trail* at 14.8 miles.

To return to Juniper Campground, follow the Caprock Coulee Nature Trail south of the road to 15.6 miles and a junction with the Scenic Drive and trailhead. Then follow a connector trail for 0.3 mile east to the *Buckhorn Trail*. Follow the Buckhorn Trail back to the campground at 17.6 miles.

In hot weather, access to the river is a luxury for most travelers. Neither river crossing is normally difficult. However, the river can be hazardous or impossible to cross if the level is high. The water is usually less than knee deep, although it can be much higher. The warm, silty water isn't ideal for a midday swim, but you can cool off by wallowing in some of the deeper pools. Channel catfish, goldeye shiners, and flathead chub live in the river.

As with any hike in the badlands, you may confuse your trail with those made by bison. Carry a compass and topographic map and know how to use them. This is a good area to watch wildlife, particularly wild turkeys, but you may also encounter ticks, prairie rattlesnakes, and poison ivy. There is no drinking water along this loop, so carry your own. If you must drink from the silty Little Missouri River, filter the water with a unit designed to remove giardia bacteria. To save wear on your filter and pump, prefilter with a double layer of coffee filters, or let the water settle overnight.

Other Theodore Roosevelt National Park Trails

The *Painted Canyon Nature Trail* (0.9 mile, South Unit) leaves from the picnic area near the Painted Canyon Visitor Center near Exit 32 off Interstate 94. The trail starts at the west end of the paved rim walkway and splits into a loop just below an area revegetated by the park (after too many hikers cut switchbacks along the trail). It then descends through badlands, passes through a juniper grove, and then winds along a grassland before climbing back to the start. The views of the South Unit from Painted Canyon are among the park's finest.

The *Painted Canyon Trail* (2.0 miles, South Unit) starts from the Painted Canyon Visitor Center and is a good place to discover some of the South Unit's 750 elk. From the visitor center start by walking east along a service road, then continue east along the canyon rim above Paddock Creek. The descent passes through several rock layers containing petrified wood, and you will travel through a small grove of cedars. The trail ends at a signed junction near the midpoint of the Upper Paddock Creek Trail.

The *Skyline Vista Trail* (0.2 mile, South Unit) is a short walk from the Scenic Loop Drive at 4.2 miles to an overlook above I-94 and the Little

Painted Canyon

Missouri River. The trail starts from the Scenic Loop Drive about four miles from the Medora Visitor Center.

The *Ridgeline Nature Trail* (0.6 mile, South Unit) is a self-guided interpretive trail that begins on the Scenic Loop Drive 10.8 miles from the Medora Visitor Center. It begins with an uphill climb and later descends on steps along a cliff. The trail explores a prairie environment, focusing on plant life and the effects of fire. Bison use this trail and may lounge in the trailhead parking area.

The *Coal Vein Nature Trail* (0.8 mile, South Unit) is an interpretive loop trail. It begins at the end of a 0.8-mile gravel road that leaves the Scenic Loop Drive 15.6 miles from the Medora Visitor Center. The loop explores an area where a seam of lignite coal burned underground from 1951 through 1977. If you ever wondered about the source of the red scoria used on so many of North Dakota's gravel roads, this is the place to find the answer. Part of the trail traverses outcroppings of bentonite clay, which is extremely slippery when wet. A shorter (0.6 mile) and more level option skips stations 4 through 10.

The *Buck Hill Trail* (0.2 mile, South Unit) begins at the end of a 0.8-mile gravel road that leaves the Scenic Loop Drive 17.1 miles from the Medora Visitor Center. The trail leads to a hilltop with a panoramic vista of the badlands above Paddock Creek. This parking area can be the start of the alternate (and shorter) version of the Upper Paddock Creek–Upper Talkington trails loop.

The *Boicourt Overlook Trail* (0.5 mile, South Unit) was completed in 2005. The trail starts at the overlook at mile point 19.9 on the Scenic Loop Drive. The first half of the former game trail is now wheelchair-accessible; the rest is an improved gravel surface. The park hopes to add benches and a viewing platform. The trail could serve as a cross-country connector to either of the Talkington trails.

The *Wind Canyon Nature Trail* (0.3 mile, South Unit) leaves from the Scenic Loop Drive 25.2 miles from the Medora Visitor Center via the Scenic Loop Drive, or it may be accessed 3.9 miles on the main road after the start of the loop. The trail leads to an overlook above the Little Missouri River.

The *CCC Trail* (1.0 mile, South Unit) connects the Jones Creek Trailhead parking area with the start of the Petrified Forest Loop Trail across the Little Missouri River. This area receives heavy use from the park's saddle horse concession. The trails near the river used by Peaceful Valley Ranch can change from year to year as the ranch varies trail ride routes.

The *Mike Auney* and *Roundup trails* (3.0 and 4.4 miles, South Unit) were opened in 1997 to provide trail access from the Roundup Group Horse Camp. The Mike Auney Trail leads from the horse camp west across the Little Missouri River to the Petrified Forest Loop Trail at a point about one-half mile north of the junction with the Lone Tree Spring Loop Trail. The Roundup Trail begins at the start of the side road to the horse camp and heads east across the Scenic Loop Drive to join the Jones Creek Trail about one-half mile west of the junction of the Jones Creek and Lower Talkington trails.

The *Lone Tree Spring Loop Trail* (6.3 miles, South Unit) shares part of the route of the Petrified Forest Loop and Maah Daah Hey trails west of the Little Missouri River. It can also be accessed 1.4 miles from Peaceful Valley on a route just south of that described for the Petrified Forest

The author in Theodore Roosevelt National Park

Loop Trail. Highlights along the way include examples of petrified wood and prairie dog towns.

The *East Boundary Horse Trail* (about 3 miles, South Unit) was opened in 1997. It begins at a horse camp at the park's east boundary. There is no public access to the trailhead for this trail, which is used primarily by a riding club.

The *Little Mo Nature Trail* (1.1 mile, North Unit) starts from the road to Juniper Campground. A shortcut between points 9 and 20 gives the option for a 0.7-mile wheelchair-accessible loop. The trail interprets the geology, flora, and fauna of the badlands along the Little Missouri River. The outer loop of the trail crosses a service road and intersects the Buckhorn Trail.

Other Adventures in Theodore Roosevelt National Park

Canoeing the Little Missouri River

For those lucky enough to catch the river at proper levels, a float trip on the Little Missouri can be one of the most memorable ways to experience Theodore Roosevelt National Park and the surrounding badlands. The Little Missouri is the only river designated as a state scenic river by North Dakota, and even a short river trip can yield a bounty of watchable wildlife and a personalized tour of the rugged badlands topography that lines the river corridor.

Catching the right season and the right year is critical. Ice on the river typically breaks up in April. Warmer temperatures and spring rains can combine to produce a float season in May or June. Predicting suitable flows is difficult. For example, in 2005 high water yielded a good season, but in the previous three springs water levels were too low for river travel. After spring runoff, low water levels will typically require far more boat dragging than floating. It is best to check water levels at the visitor center in advance of, and immediately before, your trip as water levels can change daily. River gauges are available online for Medora (http://waterdata.usgs.gov/nd/nwis/uv?06336000) and Watford City (http://waterdata.usgs.gov/nd/nwis/uv?06336000). North Dakota Parks and Recreation considers a water depth of 2.5 feet at Medora and flows of at least 250 cubic feet per second (cfs) the minimum for fair canoeing. Flows of 700 cfs at Watford City are considered good to excellent.

When water levels are sufficient, a variety of both short and longer trips are possible. Floating from Sully Creek State Park to Medora, from Medora to the I-94 Bridge, or from I-94 to Cottonwood Creek Campground can take about an hour for each section in high water, or can be a half-day trip in the lower flows typical in most years. Another option for a short trip in the North Unit is from Juniper Campground to U.S. 85 at the Long X Bridge, which usually takes about two hours. Longer trip options include the section from Medora to Elkhorn Ranch (40 miles) and Elkhorn Ranch to U.S. 85 (70 miles). The full 110 miles between the South and North Units typically requires three to four days. There are no designated launch facilities at any of these areas.

Planning for a float trip should take into account the same food, water, clothing, weather protection, and map suggestions that apply to hikers in Theodore Roosevelt National Park. Specific items needed for the river are personal flotation devices (PFDs, or life jackets to us civilians), extra paddles, buckets for bailing, dry bags or plastic bags for protecting gear, and river shoes for those inevitable shallow spots where the boat must be dragged. Be prepared for portages that will be necessary where wildlife fences have been strung across the boundaries of the national park or between private lands.

Overnight trips on the Little Missouri are a rare treat, but they add to the complexity of trip planning with vehicle shuttles and the need to find camping areas. Boaters may be able to utilize the same shuttle services as those looking to bike long sections of the Maah Daah Hey Trail. Access to the river between the North and South units of Theodore Roosevelt National Park is more difficult than it appears on maps. If you are driving the maze of gravel roads in the Dakota Prairie Grasslands, remember that new roads may be built at any time, and that road maintenance conditions can change. Roads, particularly those with any sort of grade can quickly become impassable when wet. Perhaps the best river access between the South and North units is at the Elkhorn Unit via DPG Road 2.

Riverside camping is allowed only on Dakota Prairie Grasslands or Theodore Roosevelt National Park lands. Most of the river bottom is privately held; use your map to stay on public land. If you camp on TRNP land, a free backcountry permit from a visitor center is needed. Your only option for potable water is the Maah Daah Hey's Elkhorn Camp, which is 2.5 miles from the river at Elkhorn Ranch and only has water in the summer season. Using a camp stove, and practicing Leave No Trace camping, will ensure a better trip for your group and for the others to follow. Finally, though motors are allowed on the river, their use is impractical due to shallow water and heavy silt.

The Park's Scenic Drives

For any visitor to a national park, a scenic drive is often the best option for getting an introduction to the area. For some visitors their driving trip is often their only direct experience with the park. In Theodore Roosevelt, even visitors who may venture deep into the backcountry will appreciate the front country drive for the beauty of its scenery and for the unparalleled wildlife watching. If possible take your trip near dusk or dawn, when the wildlife is most active, and traffic is light. The light for photography is also at its best. The legendary mountain photographer Galen Rowell described early morning and late evening as the "magic hour" for the effect this light had on his pictures.

For road cyclists visiting TRNP, or mountain bikers wishing to ride in the park, these scenic drives are your only options. Mountain biking is not allowed on the trails in TRNP, and the options for other road rides in the area are limited.

The South Unit Scenic Loop Drive is a 36-mile roundtrip. The park sells "A Roadlog Guide for the South and North Units" that serves as an excellent introduction to the geology of the park, as well as identifies the key features of the overlooks and nature trails found along the way. There are also five short nature trails along the loop that explore a variety of habitats and ecosystems and also lead to some of the park's most impressive overlooks.

The Scenic Loop Drive begins at the Medora Visitor Center, passes the Cottonwood Campground and reaches the start of the loop at 6.6 miles. At 24.9 miles from the visitor center, a spur leads north to Roundup Group Horse Camp, then north out of the park. The loop then passes Peaceful Valley and closes at 29.1 miles. Another 6.6 miles will return you to Medora. Short (0.8 mile each) gravel side roads lead to nature trails and overlooks at Coal Vein and Buck Hill at 15.6 and 17.1 miles, respectively. In 2005, much of the loop road was repaved.

For me, the highlight of the Scenic Loop Drive is seeing the South Unit's herd of wild horses. There is no better symbol of the west than a wild stallion and his closely guarded herd roaming through the deep draws and steep hillsides of the badlands. These small bands of horses move frequently, so consider yourself lucky if you do observe them. Both bison and prairie dogs, two other icons of the west, are much easier to spot along the way. Mule deer, pronghorn, and elk are more likely to be seen near sunrise or sunset. Listen quietly and enjoy the sounds of birds chirping, prairie dogs yipping, and the bark of a distant coyote.

The North Unit Scenic Drive leads 13.7 miles from the Entrance Station to a dead end near Oxbow Overlook, high above the Little Missouri River on the western edge of the park. The North Unit Visitor Center is located at 0.1 mile, and the turnoff to the Juniper Campground is at 4.6 miles. There are ten other pullouts along the way. The most spectacular of these is Riverbend Overlook and shelter at 7.8 miles, built by the Civilian Conservation Corps in 1937. The overlook is the site of most of the calendar shots taken in the North Unit. The road closes in winter at the trailhead for the Caprock Coulee Nature Trail.

Elkhorn Ranch Unit
A visit to the Elkhorn Ranch Unit of Theodore Roosevelt National Park takes travelers through some of the most remote parts of the Little Missouri badlands. But this trip to the site of one of Roosevelt's primary residences is well worth the time and effort. No buildings remain at the site, but exhibits show the site of Roosevelt's house and other ranch structures. The site is still so quiet and remote one can imagine

approaching the ranch to find the future president sitting on the shaded porch, serenaded by the rustle of wind through cottonwoods.

Ask at any visitor center for a copy of the map showing the ranch layout and the access to it. You can reach Elkhorn Ranch using the directions for the Maah Daah Hey Trail Elkhorn Camp, which is 2.0 miles west of the ranch site. TRNP also suggests access from the west via Exit 10 off I-94. Drive 15 miles on County Road 11, 11 miles north on DPG Road 708, then 3 miles east on DPG Road FH2.

Access to the ranch from the east side of the Little Missouri River is more difficult, and requires fording the river. From the Scenic Loop Drive, drive north past Roundup Group Horse Camp out of TRNP to reach unpaved DPG Road 702. It is 22 miles from the Scenic Loop Drive to the junction with the Blacktail Road (DPG Road FH2), and another 2 miles to the river, opposite the Elkhorn Ranch Site. Alternatively, this point can be reached from U.S. 85 at the Fairfield town site by following the Blacktail Road (DPG Road FH2) for 23 miles.

Maah Daah Hey
Trail

HIDDEN IN A remote corner of western North Dakota is one of the country's most spectacular single tracks. Here is the chance to ride rugged badlands, hike through scenic parks filled with wildlife, and enjoy it all without the crowds. It is because we have enjoyed this trail so much, and because of the growing interest in the recreation opportunities in the region, that this guidebook exists.

The 96-mile Maah Daah Hey Trail connects the North and South units of Theodore Roosevelt National Park through the badlands and grasslands of the Dakota Prairie Grasslands. The trail was originally conceived by horse riders seeking a long, challenging route across the badlands, but the trail is also open to hikers. Mountain bikers, who may now be the most frequent trail users, can ride the trail except in the two units of Theodore Roosevelt National Park, where the route crosses two designated wilderness areas. The Buffalo Gap Trail bypasses the park's South Unit, but there is currently no formal bypass route for bikers around the North Unit. The trail is managed as a cooperative effort between North Dakota Parks and Recreation, Theodore Roosevelt National Park (TRNP), and the Dakota Prairie Grasslands (DPG) of the United States Forest Service.

Though the Little Missouri badlands are not as isolated as they were in Theodore Roosevelt's time, the scenery remains every bit as captivating. Much of the trail passes through well-developed badlands landscapes, where bizarre landforms vie with fossil wood and eye-grabbing vistas for the traveler's attention. Wildlife watchers will enjoy frequent

MAP D: Maah Daah Hey Trail and the Little Missouri National Grasslands

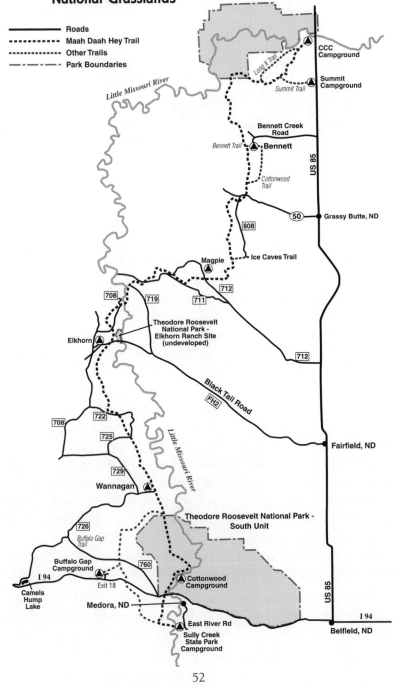

Roads
Maah Daah Hey Trail
Other Trails
Park Boundaries

Little Missouri River

Long X Trail

CCC Campground

Summit Trail

Summit Campground

Bennett Creek Road

Bennett Trail

Bennett

US 85

Cottonwood Trail

50

Grassy Butte, ND

808

Ice Caves Trail

Magpie

712

708

719

711

Theodore Roosevelt National Park - Elkhorn Ranch Site (undeveloped)

Elkhorn

712

Black Tail Road

FH2

Fairfield, ND

708

722

725

Little Missouri River

729

Wannagan

Theodore Roosevelt National Park - South Unit

726

Buffalo Gap Trail

760

US 85

Buffalo Gap Campground

I 94

Exit 18

Camels Hump Lake

Cottonwood Campground

Medora, ND

East River Rd

I 94

Belfield, ND

Sully Creek State Park Campground

Table 2: Maah Daah Hey Trail Mileage

	South to North Distance	Interval Distance	Section Distance
Sully Creek State Park	0.0	0.0	
Buffalo Gap Trail South End	2.3	2.3	
Enter TRNP South Unit	5.1	2.8	
Ford to Cottonwood Campground	7.0	1.9	
Trail to Peaceful Valley	8.2	1.2	
Lone Tree Spring Loop Trail	8.6	3.5	
Petrified Forest Loop Trail	10.2	1.6	
Leave TRNP South Unit	13.5	3.3	
Buffalo Gap Trail North End	13.9	0.4	
Cross DPG Road 726	16.8	2.9	
Wannagan Camp (0.2 mile west)	17.1	0.3	
Cross DPG Road 728	20.4	3.3	3.3
Crooked Creek	24.0	3.6	6.9
Cross DPG Road 725	24.7	0.7	7.6
Roosevelt Creek	27.5	2.8	10.4
Cross DPG Road 722	29.5	2.0	12.4
Dry Creek	33.7	4.2	16.6
Ellison Creek	36.0	2.3	18.9
Elkhorn Camp (0.3 mile west)	38.5	2.5	21.4
TRNP Elkhorn Ranch Site	40.0	1.5	1.5
South Crossing DPG Road 708	41.7	1.7	3.2
North Crossing DPG Road 708	45.5	3.8	7.0
Ford Little Missouri River	46.8	1.3	8.3
DPG Road 712	50.0	3.2	11.5
Pond	52.3	2.3	13.8
Devils Pass	53.3	1.0	14.8
Pond	54.5	1.3	16.0
Cross DPG Road 711	55.0	0.5	16.5
Magpie Camp (0.3 mile north)	58.2	3.2	19.7
Ice Caves Trail	61.4	3.2	3.2
DPG Road 809 and Pond	67.5	6.1	9.3
Beicegel Creek	68.0	0.5	9.8
DPG Road 809	71.8	3.8	13.6

Continued on next page

Table 2: Continued

	South to North Distance	Interval Distance	Section Distance
McKenzie County Road 50	72.5	0.8	14.3
Cottonwood Trail (7.1 miles to Bennett Tr.)	75.0	2.5	16.8
Cottonwood Creek	76.5	1.5	18.3
Bennett Camp (3.1 miles east)	80.0	3.5	21.8
China Wall	81.0	1.0	1.0
DPG Road 823 near Bennett Creek	82.3	1.3	2.3
Pond at Collar Draw	84.8	2.5	4.8
Enter TRNP North Unit	86.0	1.2	6.0
Leave TRNP North Unit	88.0	2.0	8.0
DPG Road 825 and west end Long X Trail	91.0	3.0	11.0
Summit Trail	93.5	2.5	13.5
Long X Trail, east end	95.5	2.0	15.5
CCC Campground	96.0	0.5	16.0

sightings of pronghorn, along with the opportunity to spot bison, elk, bighorn sheep, and wild turkey. The trail is remote enough that it is possible to spend all day on the trail and not see other people.

The name Maah Daah Hey, and the trail's turtle symbol come from the Mandan Indians. "Maah Daah Hey" means an area that has been or will be around for a long time. The turtle is a symbol of determination, steadfastness, patience, and fortitude. The theme of longevity and permanence are ideal for a trail through a landscape unaltered by settlement of the west, and leading through a national park dedicated to preserving Roosevelt's conservation legacy.

The trail is marked with 4" x 6" wooden posts branded with a turtle emblem, though to many cynics, the emblem resembles a tick. There are now mileposts along the entire trail. Though a few short sections of trail follow older two-track dirt roads, most of the trail in the Dakota Prairie Grasslands was built as new single track. Generally, the trail is well worn and easy to follow, though it is possible to get misled by cattle paths that cross the trail. In 2003, the Maah Daah Hey Trail was designated a National Recreation Trail, an honor that brings no extra funding or protection, but does bring higher national visibility to the trail.

The Dakota Prairie Grasslands has constructed four camps at Wannagan, Elkhorn, Magpie, and Bennett, about 20 miles apart along the trail. These fenced campgrounds offer vault toilets, campsites with fire rings and picnic tables, and most importantly, water wells. The wells are operated by pumps that are turned on during the summer season, and normally run from around May 1 to December 1. Please check with the DPG to ensure the pumps are working before you start your trip. Three of the four camps are on short side trails off the Maah Daah Hey Trail. However, Bennett Camp is located three miles from the main trail. Elkhorn and Magpie have some shaded sites, but some will find Wannagan fairly stark and shadeless.

Backcountry camping is permitted anywhere on the Dakota Prairie Grasslands. However, private and state-owned sections of the Maah Daah Hey Trail are off-limits to camping, and travelers are confined to the trail in these sections. Those planning to stay in either unit of Theodore Roosevelt National Park must obtain a free backcountry permit.

The Maah Daah Hey Trail crosses both units of Theodore Roosevelt National Park. These park lands are designated wilderness areas, so mountain bikes are prohibited. Because there is no alternative route on public land around the North Unit, there is currently no designated bypass for mountain bikers. However, the DPG and the Maah Daah Hey Trail Association are negotiating with a landowner south of the park to acquire a right-of-way through private land for the trail. Bikers can leave the trail on the Cottonwood or Bennett trails or north of milepost (MP) 82 on DPG Road 823 and rejoin it at MP 91 on DPG 825. Check with the DPG before planning a ride around the North Unit. For the park's South Unit, the DPG has constructed the 20-mile Buffalo Gap Trail, which bypasses the Maah Daah Hey Trail from the Sully Creek Campground to the grassland north of the South Unit of TRNP, and also connects to the DPG Buffalo Gap Campground. This campground has coin-operated showers, one of the few in USFS campgrounds.

Though the Maah Daah Hey Trail was designed and built as a point-to-point trail, most trail users prefer loop routes for their one-day trips.

After all why cover the same trail twice when you could be covering new ground all day long? Thanks to the construction of new side trails to the MDH there are several possible loops using the MDH, plus a few other options for those who don't mind riding a bit of gravel road. Hikers and horse riders have the option of combining the Buffalo Gap and Maah Daah Hey trails for a 31.6-mile loop. Those that don't mind a bit of riding or hiking on roads with low traffic can combine the Maah Daah Hey and Ice Caves trails with ten miles of DPG roads 808 and 809 for a 22-mile loop. The new Cottonwood and Bennett trails can be combined with the MDH for a 15.4-mile loop. Hikers and horse riders again have the option to combine the MDH with a road route that bypasses the North Unit of Theodore Roosevelt National Park. Finally, the Long X Trail can be combined with the last five miles of the Maah Daah Hey Trail for the 11-mile loop that is especially popular with horse parties.

While often very scenic, the DPG segments of the Maah Daah Hey Trail do not offer the wilderness experience found in TRNP. Parts of the trail pass through active oil and gas fields. Trail users should give well

Maah Daah Hey, south trailhead

facilities a wide berth due to hazards from poisonous gasses. The other main use of the grasslands is cattle grazing, an activity popular since Roosevelt's time. The signs of cattle will be all around you. Their paths may obscure the official trail, and their muddy hoof prints often make rough riding. However, it is important to realize that the grasslands is a multiple-use area. It is the energy firms and the counties that maintain most of the access roads under permit or easements, and it is the cattle ranchers that maintain the stock tanks and dams.

Long distance travelers on the Maah Daah Hey Trail will face two main obstacles. The first challenges are two fords of the Little Missouri River, one at the south end in Sully Creek State Park, and the other near the midpoint of the trail. In many years, the river can be easily forded on hard bottom by late spring. However, in very wet years, the river may be impassable, except by boat, late into the summer. It is wise to check on river levels with either the DPG or TRNP if you are planning a trip that requires a river crossing.

Perversely, the traveler's other obstacle is lack of drinking water. In addition to the wells at the four designated camps, the Maah Daah Hey Trail crosses some major creeks large enough to hold water into the summer, but these creeks are unreliable. Other options are the year-round springs and seasonal stock ponds and tanks in the DPG used to water cattle in summer. The DPG's MDH trail map shows the locations of the year-round flowing wells and springs. This water is often unappetizing in appearance and could be undrinkable after the cattle are brought from their winter pastures to the grasslands. If you are forced to rely on this water, look for the intake pipe to the stock tanks; it may be possible to get fresher water here. Remember that any water you find along the trail must be treated before drinking.

Another tactic is to stash caches of water at places where all-season gravel roads cross the trail. For example, a water cache at McKenzie County Road 50 requires a small amount of driving, and fills a long gap in the trail between Magpie Creek and Bennett Creek. If you set up a cache, remember your Leave No Trace practices and haul out everything that you've carried in. The DPG also plans to add more directional signs along the trail to help travelers more easily find flowing wells.

The Maah Daah Hey Trail is perhaps most popular with mountain bikers. The trail is ideal for experienced riders. The combination of wild landforms and wide open spaces is unmatched by any other biking trail. The trail has a good mix of challenging, technical single track across the rugged badlands and easy cruising along the flat, grassy tablelands. Their greater range gives mountain bikers fewer water problems than long-distance hikers or horse riders.

To cover all of the Maah Daah Hey Trail most groups will need to arrange a shuttle from one end to the other. Dakota Cyclery in Medora offers a variety of shuttle services ranging from day trips on the MDH and Buffalo Gap trails, to fully supported end-to-end trips. Several other outfitters in the area offer shuttle services in season. Backpackers looking to cover the MDH in two trips could use the strategy my wife and I followed to complete the trail. For the north half of the trail we left our vehicle at the CCC Campground and were shuttled to DPG Road 712. After a quick side trip to the Little Missouri River we hiked to the north end of the trail. For the south half we were shuttled to DPG Road 708 then again walked back to our vehicle, after taking a side trip to the

Maah Daah Hey Trail vista

river. This approach eliminates the need for the middle ford of the Little Missouri River.

Severe wind and cold during winter and the hot, dry heat of summer will likely ensure that the Maah Daah Hey Trail receives more use in the spring and fall. At any time of year be prepared for extremes of temperature, sun, and wind. There are also many stretches of trail across gumbo, a remarkably sticky and heavy type of clay that is impassable when wet. It is better to wait a few hours for the trail to dry than to attempt to ride it when wet. The western Dakotas are one of the country's least populated regions. Keep in mind that you're on your own in these badlands.

The DPG's Maah Daah Hey trail builders may not yet be done. They are working on plans to extend the trail 40 miles south to Burning Coal Vein Campground northwest of Amidon, North Dakota. The trail would use land owned by the DPG, the State of North Dakota, and the Theodore Roosevelt Medora Foundation. A new campground near Coal Creek and a side trail could be added if the project is approved. The campsite would be accessed from DPG Road FH3 and have facilities, including a water well, similar to those at existing Maah Daah Hey camps. The extension project is currently undergoing review under the National Environmental Policy Act.

Sully Creek Campground (DPG Road 3) to Wannagan Camp (DPG Road 726)

Sully Creek State Park, Medora Ranger District, and Theodore Roosevelt National Park, South Unit

Description: Exciting terrain, a variety of scenery, many fossils, and prolific wildlife make this a popular trip. The trail through the South Unit of TRNP is closed to mountain bikes.

General Location: Three miles south of Medora, North Dakota.

Highlight: A scenic trail through one of America's best wildlife viewing parks.

Access: To reach *Sully Creek State Park* from Medora, turn south from Pacific Ave. onto East River Road South. After 0.5 mile, the road turns to gravel. At 1.9 miles, turn right onto 36th Street at a sign for the park. There is parking at 2.8 miles at the beginning of the campground loop. The Maah Daah Hey Trail in Theodore Roosevelt National Park can also be reached from the north side of the Exit 24 interchange from I-94. Look for a crawl hole next to a locked gate in the bison fence. *Wannagan Camp* can be reached from I-94 off Exit 23, three miles west of Medora. From Exit 23, turn north on gravel DPG Road 730. At 5.2 miles a road to the TRNP Petrified Forest Westgate Trailhead splits right. At 7.9 miles, cross the Buffalo Gap Trail. At 9.7 miles turn right onto DPG Road 726, which may not be signed. At 15.8 miles keep right at the intersection with Road 729. At 16.6 miles, turn left onto gravel DPG Road 726-15 which leads to the camp at 16.9 miles. Another option is a more direct route to Wannagan Camp from Exit 10 off I-94 that follows DPG Road 726 for 14 miles.

Distance: 17.1 miles one way.

Maps: DPG Maah Daah Hey Trail Map, Trails Illustrated Theodore Roosevelt National Park (#259), USGS Medora and Wannagan Creek East, ND 7.5-minute quadrangles, and Map D, *page 52.*

The southern section of the Maah Daah Hey Trail is perhaps its most diverse. Sully Creek State Park, Theodore Roosevelt National Park, and the Dakota Prairie Grasslands have combined to build a trail that highlights the best that the North Dakota badlands can offer. On this section you'll visit the trail's three main ecosystems: the lush river bottoms along the Little Missouri, stark badlands, and the surprisingly productive grasslands that surround them. The trip through the South Unit of TRNP is one of the country's best wildlife walks. You'll likely see prairie dogs, bison, and pronghorn here, and possibly coyotes, deer, or elk as well.

The trail through the South Unit is closed to mountain bikes. Most of the South Unit, west of the Little Missouri River, is a designated wilderness area where mechanized travel is not permitted. To remedy this situation, the DPG has built the Buffalo Gap Trail as a bypass route around the wilderness.

The Maah Daah Hey Trail begins in Sully Creek State Park at the signboard and parking area near the campground entrance. Follow the wooden posts that mark the trail between the campground and the Little Missouri River to a ford that is located near horse sites 3 and 4. During most years, this crossing of the sandy bottom is relatively safe and easy by late spring. In other years, high water makes the crossing dangerous until well into summer. Be sure to ask about water levels with the South Unit of TRNP, or get the data from the USGS water gauge data at Medora before committing to a river ford. The website is water-data.usgs.gov/nwis and station #06336000 is the Little Missouri River at Medora.

After one-quarter mile of sandy trail on private land on the west bank of the river, the trail crosses a two-track dirt road at a sign for a guest ranch. To help gauge your progress, there are mileposts along the entire trail. Next, head west to a fence line where the trail begins a gradual climb up a small draw, then enters some well-developed badlands.

Trail marker and Table Rock

Continue to climb until reaching the signed junction with the south end of the *Buffalo Gap Trail* at 2.3 miles at the crest of a divide. Here the Buffalo Gap Trail turns west, and an unofficial mountain bike route leads east, while the Maah Daah Hey Trail dives north off the divide. The trail will climb over one more divide before reaching the west end of Pacific Avenue at Exit 24 from I-94 at 5.1 miles. In 2006 the DPG plans to relocate part of the trail between the Buffalo Gap junction and I-94 to both lessen grades on the trail and to avoid bighorn sheep habitat.

Walk around the east side of the interchange and look for a pullout near a hole in the bison fence that marks the TRNP boundary. Once in the park, remember to give any wildlife a wide berth. It is likely that you will see bison grazing along the flat river bottom. At 7.0 miles, Cottonwood Campground is on the east side of the river across a normally easy ford. Turn west over a small divide to reach a junction with the southern of two feeder trails from Peaceful Valley Ranch at 8.2 miles. The feeder trail leads east 0.8 mile to a river ford opposite the horse camp. Walk west up the valley of Knutson Creek past some appealing campsites to a junction with the *Lone Tree Spring Loop Trail* at 8.6 miles. The Maah Daah Hey Trail bears right to follow the east side of the loop on a 400-foot climb to Petrified Forest Plateau. Before reaching the plateau, keep left at 9.9 miles and the junction with the northern feeder trail to Peaceful Valley. From this junction to the north end of the Petrified Forest Loop, the Maah Daah Hey Trail follows the Petrified Forest Loop as described in the TRNP chapter.

The last bit of climbing leads to the junction with the *Petrified Forest Loop Trail* at 10.2 miles. Keep right to follow the loop across this remarkably level area. The plateau is great for watching bison and other wildlife. At 10.7 miles the *Mike Auney Trail* leads right 3.0 miles across the Little Missouri River to Roundup Group Horse Camp. The Maah Daah Hey Trail next leads onto a narrow ridge offering tremendous badlands views. At 13.4 miles, reach the junction where the Maah Daah Hey Trail leaves the Petrified Forest Loop at its north end. At 13.5 miles, exit the park at a gate through the bison fence.

Once out of the park, the trail drops on switchbacks to the signed intersection with the *Buffalo Gap Trail* on the south end of a stock dam at 13.9 miles. On the far end of the pond is milepost 14. The Maah Daah Hey Trail continues across state land through another mile of badlands, and then follows a side draw toward Wannagan Creek. A few flat shaded spots along the draw could serve as dry campsites. Reach a signed crossing of Wannagan Creek, and then cross gravel DPG Road 726 at 16.8 miles. Climb to a narrow ridge top to reach the signed junction with the *Wannagan Camp Trail* at 17.1 miles. Wannagan Camp is visible 0.2 mile to the west from this junction.

Wannagan Camp (DPG Road 726) to Elkhorn Camp (DPG Road F-12)

Medora Ranger District

Description: A challenging trail for hikers and mountain bikes through rolling grasslands and spectacular badlands.

General Location: Fourteen miles northwest of Medora, North Dakota.

Highlight: Scenic badlands are located at Ellison Creek and south of Crooked Creek.

Access: Good maps are essential for reaching both trailheads. *Wannagan Camp* can be reached from I-94 off Exit 23 three miles west of Medora. From Exit 23, turn north on gravel DPG Road 730. At 5.2 miles keep left where a road to the TRNP Petrified Forest Westgate Trailhead splits right. At 7.9 miles cross the Buffalo Gap Trail. At 9.7 miles turn right onto DPG Road 726, which may not be signed. At 15.8 miles, keep right at the intersection with DPG Road 729. At 16.6 miles, turn left onto gravel DPG Road 726-15, which leads to the camp at 16.9 miles. Another option is a more direct route to Wannagan Camp from Exit 10 off I-94 that follows DPG Road 726 for 14 miles. *Elkhorn Camp* can be reached by turning north on DPG Road 729 from Road 726. However, this road may not receive much maintenance and may be slick when

Horses, biker, and hiker at Wannagan Camp

wet until it intersects gravel DPG Road 728. Stay left on Road 729 at the Road 728 junction, and then turn right onto gravel DPG Road 725. Next turn left onto gravel DPG Road 722, followed by a right turn onto gravel DPG Road 708. Road 708 leads in about 3.5 miles to a right turn onto DPG Road FH2, which leads to Elkhorn Camp in one mile, and the Elkhorn Ranch Unit of Theodore Roosevelt National Park in three miles. The 0.3-mile Elkhorn Trail connects the camp to the Maah Daah Hey Trail. The Maah Daah Hey Trail crosses this access route on both roads 722 and 725, offering two opportunities to cache water. TRNP recommends a 27-mile long route to Elkhorn from I-94 at Exit 10 via County Road 11 and DPG Road 708.

Distance: 21.4 miles one way.

Maps: DPG Maah Daah Hey Trail Map; Trails Illustrated Theodore Roosevelt National Park (#259); USGS Wannagan Creek East, Wannagan Creek West, and Roosevelt Creek West, ND, 7.5-minute quadrangles; and Map D, *page 52.*

Like much of the Maah Daah Hey Trail, the Wannagan to Elkhorn traverse challenges hikers with a long section without reliable water. At the same time it lures mountain bikers and horse riders with the promise of uncrowded single track, and with two scenic badlands areas sandwiched around a remote center of rolling grassland. Few hikers will be able to make this crossing in a single day, but with the exception of the attractive sites at Crooked Creek, and the unappealing sites near Roosevelt Creek, camping and water options are few. However, caching water where the trail crosses DPG roads 725 or 722 will allow campers the luxury of choosing any site they please.

Early season visitors will find more tracks from pronghorns than humans. As with all sections of the Maah Daah Hey Trail, make sure that the water pumps are on at the camps before you head out, and keep an eye on the weather. Rain or damp conditions quickly turn the trail muddy. At its worst, even a short stretch of gumbo can be slick and sticky enough to stop bikers, horses, or hikers in their tracks. The weather here is more of a challenge than the terrain. Since the only settings on North Dakota's thermostat are freeze and fry, there's little chance you'll be traveling in ideal conditions.

Biker leaving Wannagan Camp

From the junction of the Maah Daah Hey Trail and the 0.2-mile side trail to Wannagan Camp at 17.1 miles, the trail heads north with a steep, spectacular climb up switchbacks to the ridge that dominates the view east from the camp. The next two miles feature an exquisite ridge-top traverse high above the Wannagan Creek badlands where partly submerged stumps of petrified wood litter the trail. The trail next turns north and drops into a pleasant, protected draw before crossing gravel DPG Road 728 at 20.4 miles. The trail uses a few switchbacks to drop into another small draw north of MP 21 where camping is possible.

North of this draw, the Maah Daah Hey Trail traverses west along the crest of a thin ridge with exceptional badlands vistas. North of this ridge, however, the trail begins to move further west of the Little Missouri River so that badlands formations are not as well developed. However, the trail soon crosses Crooked Creek and reaches flat and scenic campsites at MP 24. Here you are likely to see more wild turkey than cattle, and a bit of exploration should reveal a few pieces of petrified wood. If you have cached water at DPG Road 725, this is your best option for camping.

The Maah Daah Hey Trail next climbs to cross DPG Road 725 at 24.7 miles and begins a long traverse of open grassland. While gradually descending toward Roosevelt Creek, the trail passes both a remarkably huge stock dam and an active oil well to the east of the trail. The north bank of Roosevelt Creek offers small campsites in the trees, but will probably have cattle in summer. The cattle are likely attracted by the flowing well and stock tank found at the signed creek crossing at 27.5 miles. The wide crossing can be muddy. From Roosevelt Creek, the trail climbs to a ridge overlooking a new road leading to an oil well before dropping to cross gravel DPG Road 722 at 29.5 miles.

Hike alongside DPG Road 722 before climbing north to a ridge top and two-track road that leads to a stock tank found shortly before MP 30. Continue on the ridge top to cross a new gravel road to an oil well. Switchback off the ridge to reach the bottom of a small draw at MP 32. Climb from the draw to reach another stock tank near the intersection with some faint ranch roads. After a short time on the divide, descend toward Dry Creek. The south fork of Dry Creek is a long, narrow gash in the earth, an erosional feature more typical of South Dakota's Badlands National Park than of the Little Missouri badlands. Here the process of stream erosion has acted swiftly and violently to carve a deep, straight channel through soft bedrock. Cross signed Dry Creek at 33.7 miles. The creek bottom is too dry and narrow for camping.

After Dry Creek, the Maah Daah Hey Trail moves closer to the Little Missouri River, and again passes through well-developed badlands terrain. There is a faint ranch road on the next divide north, and a stock dam and grassy two-track road in the following draw. Cross over one gentler divide to reach the signed crossing of Ellison Creek at MP 36. Hike east down the creek, then turn left up a side draw at a large stock pond. Enjoy views of the surrounding badlands and reach the signed junction with the Elkhorn Trail at 38.5 miles. The *Elkhorn Trail* turns left here to reach Elkhorn Camp alongside DPG Road FH2 in 0.3 mile.

Elkhorn Camp (DPG Road F-12) to Magpie Camp (DPG Road 712)

Medora Ranger District

Description: A pleasant walk or ride through the Buckhorn and Devils Pass Oil Fields.

General Location: About 36 miles northwest of Medora, North Dakota.

Highlight: Theodore Roosevelt's Elkhorn Ranch Site, and the spectacular crossing of Devils Pass.

Access: *Elkhorn Camp* can be reached by continuing north on DPG Road 729 (this road may not receive much maintenance and may be slick when wet) from Wannagan Camp to the intersection with gravel DPG Road 728. Stay left on Road 729 at this junction, then turn right onto gravel DPG Road 725. Next turn left onto gravel DPG Road 722 followed by a right turn onto gravel DPG Road 708. Road 708 leads in about 3.5

miles to a right turn onto DPG Road FH2, which leads to Elkhorn Camp in 1.0 mile and the Elkhorn Ranch Unit of Theodore Roosevelt National Park in 3.0 miles. The 0.3-mile Elkhorn Trail connects the camp to the Maah Daah Hey Trail. TRNP recommends a 27-mile long route to the Elkhorn Camp from I-94 Exit 10 via County Road 11 and DPG Road 708. The nearest road access to the Little Missouri River crossing is from DPG Road 708. *Magpie Camp* can be found by driving west on DPG Road 712 (Magpie Road) from U.S. 85 about 3.5 miles north of the town site of Fairfield. Keep right on Road 712 at an intersection with Road 711. Road 712 will cross the Maah Daah Hey Trail about one-half mile before DPG Road 7124 branches right to the camp about 15.5 miles from U.S. 85.

Distance: 19.7 miles one way.

Maps: DPG Maah Daah Hey Trail Map; Trails Illustrated Theodore Roosevelt National Park (#259); USGS Roosevelt Creek West, Eagle Draw, Hanks Gully, and Squaretop Butte, ND 7.5-minute quadrangles; and Map D, *page 52.*

Maah Daah Hey Trail with horses, riders and hiker

This section of the Maah Daah Hey Trail around the Little Missouri River is one of the most diverse. Much of the trail is intertwined with a maze of gravel roads that service the area oil wells, but the trail makes up for this intrusion with some nice campsites, and perhaps its most scenic feature: the rough and narrow crossing of Devils Pass. Here is also perhaps the trail's biggest obstacle, the crossing of the Little Missouri River. Most years the crossing is nothing worse than a place to get your feet wet. However, during the spring runoff river levels are uncertain. It is best to check with the staff at Theodore Roosevelt National Park to make sure the water is not too high. North of Whitetail Creek water is scarce, but parties with the ability to navigate through the maze of grasslands roads will find several options for caching water.

During his ranching days Theodore Roosevelt kept his main ranch at Elkhorn, just south of the midpoint of the Maah Daah Hey Trail. The site is preserved as part of TRNP, but has not been developed. A map of the Elkhorn Ranch site with driving directions is available from TRNP visitor centers.

The section begins at the junction of the Maah Daah Hey and Elkhorn trails. Elkhorn Camp is 0.3 mile to the west along the *Elkhorn Trail* at MP 38.5. From the junction, the Maah Daah Hey heads north to cross gravel DPG Road FH2. The trail crosses a two-track dirt road near MP 39, then closely follows Road 2. At MP 40 the trail reaches the edge of the bottomland along the Little Missouri River next to an unmarked parking area for the Elkhorn Ranch Unit of Theodore Roosevelt National Park. At MPs 39 and 40, flowing wells are located just south and east of the trail.

The Elkhorn Ranch Unit of TRNP is undeveloped, but visitors are welcome to wander the area. A gate in the National Park Service fence at the parking area leads to a mowed path. By taking a left at a T-junction, this path will lead to the ranch and blacksmith site near the river. Roosevelt described his home ranch as a "long, low house of hewn logs" with a line of cottonwoods in front for shade. He described the ranch as always cool and pleasant during the fierce heat of summer, and choked with blazing fires to thwart winter's iron desolation. Roosevelt was an active rancher,

The Maah Daah Hey Trail north of Wannagan Camp

joining his men in the chores of riding, roping, and roundup. He was active in stockowners groups, giving early warnings against the perils of overgrazing, and forecasted the devastation that the winter of 1886–1887 would wreak on the cattle herds.

From MP 40, the Maah Daah Hey Trail turns north and climbs above the river. There is a stock tank in a small draw near MP 41, and another spring-fed tank just before the trail makes its first crossing of DPG Road 708. The trail follows the east side of Road 708 for a quarter mile before turning north at MP 42 to drop into pretty Morgan Draw. The trail follows down the draw to cross a gravel road that leads to an oil well at a feeding station for cattle. Continue past a flowing well and stock tank, and then down the draw, past MP 44 before beginning the 200-foot climb up to a flat, windswept tableland.

Head northeast across the tableland and pass an old corral before dropping to the second, more northern crossing on DPG Road 708 at 45.5 miles. This is the closest road access to the trail's crossing of the Little Missouri River. Descend on switchbacks to the river bottomland at

MP 46 where shaded camping is possible. Turn north and reach the ford of the Little Missouri at 46.8 miles. On the west bank bluffs look for a prominent black lignite layer in the exposed bedrock and for pieces of lignite in the river gravels.

On the east side of the river, a sign indicates that the trail will cross private land for the next quarter mile. Cross through a self-closing gate onto state land where you are required to stay on the trail for the next one-half mile. Reach MP 47 just before a signed crossing of Whitetail Creek. In high water, this crossing could be difficult and wet.

Hike along the north bank of the creek through a pretty grove of cottonwood trees. After you cross onto the DPG, look for potential campsites in the trees that offer shade and fresh water, a combination that will be difficult to match in the next few miles. Turn left and away from the creek before reaching MP 48. Beyond MP 48, cross through a self-closing gate, then reach DPG Road 719. Cross the road after an oil-well service road branches north and begin to climb.

Near the top of the steep route full of switchbacks is a stainless steel post indicating the midpoint of the Maah Daah Hey Trail at MP 49. The post lists the names of trail coordinator Curt Glasoe, crew chief Russ Walsh, and the crew that constructed the trail. Enjoy your last view of the river on this section and head north on a high plateau. Cross through another self-closing gate on a very narrow ridge line before reaching MP 50 near an oil well alongside DPG Road 712.

North Dakota's oil fields are part of a geologic structure called the Williston Basin, a 300,000-square-mile feature centered in the western part of the state. Oil was first discovered here in 1951. Production and exploration have followed the same ups and downs common to the rest of the energy industry with bursts of activity following advances in technology, new discoveries, and events such as the 1970s OPEC oil embargo. Over half the oil comes from rocks of the Mississippian Madison Group, very similar to the rocks that make up the Limestone Plateau in South Dakota's Black Hills. North Dakota's statewide production of 80,000 barrels a day is relatively minor, even in this age of declining domestic production. While the top producing state of Texas yields over one million barrels daily, matching the total imported into the

Author on the Elkhorn Ranch Trail

United States from Venezuela, North Dakota's rate barely matches what we import from the Caribbean nation of Trinidad and Tobago.

Hike east beside DPG Road 712, before winding south around a small butte and then crossing the road. After the road turns north, veer away from it to the west to cross a small ridge in a section marked by patches of gumbo and the signs of an old burn. Recross DPG Road 712 and reach a small pond at 52.3 miles. A grove of juniper and aspen on the far side of the pond could make a nice campsite. The trail next traverses the edge of a plateau high above the rugged Whitetail Creek badlands. Reach a junction with a well-worn two-track road at a swing gate and a sign for Devils Pass at 53.3 miles. The pass is a narrow sliver of upland that is the only connection between the badlands along Whitetail Creek to the south and those along Magpie Creek to the north. Leave the road to the left and make the crossing of the narrow pass while enjoying the views of the steep, rugged badlands on either side.

Soon recross the old two-track road and then pass a dry stock dam. At 54.5 miles is a small dam with water and a potential campsite down the trail. Climb from the pond up to DPG Road 711 near the junction with a large Exxon Oil Well and DPG Road 711-6. Cross DPG Road 711 and pass MP 55 in a narrow, shaded draw. There is a spring-fed stock tank just south of the trail before crossing another self-closing gate. Crest a small divide to reach a stock pond just south of MP 56. Next, cross DPG Road 712-10 and pass MP 57, which lies just south of a tiny butte. Pass a huge oil well, then cross the access road to another, before reaching DPG Road 712 at 57.7 miles, just east of a split in the road and a cattle guard. Enter the wide valley of Magpie Creek and continue east to reach the side trail to Magpie Camp at 58.2 miles. *The Magpie Trail* turns north to reach the campground in 0.3 mile.

The Little Missouri badlands have a scenic beauty all their own. The landscape is a mix of shortgrass prairie and seemingly barren badlands. It is a terrain that combines sweeping vistas with often overlooked wildflowers, rock formations, and wildlife among the sculpted coulees and grassy tablelands. The grasslands is a chaotic patchwork of public and private land. Thus it cannot support the diversity of wildlife seen in Theodore Roosevelt National Park, but mule deer, pronghorn, coyotes, and prairie dogs are common. Lucky visitors might spy rare elk or bighorn sheep.

Magpie Camp (DPG Road 712)
to Bennett Camp

Medora and McKenzie Ranger Districts

Description: A long, lonely mix of prairie and badlands open to hikers, mountain bikes, and horses.

General Location: Eight miles west of Grassy Butte, North Dakota.

Highlight: A remote setting sprinkled with many petrified wood deposits.

Access: *Magpie Camp* can be found by driving west on DPG Road 712 (Magpie Road) from U.S. 85 about 3.5 miles north of the town site of Fairfield. Keep right on Road 712 at an intersection with DPG Road 711. Road 712 will cross the Maah Daah Hey Trail about one-half mile before DPG Road 7124 branches right to the camp about 15.5 miles from U.S. 85. McKenzie County Road 50 (DPG Road 7, also called the Beicegel Creek Road) leaves U.S. 85 15.5 miles south of the entrance to the North Unit of TRNP at the small community of Grassy Butte. The road is paved for at least seven miles west to the crossing of the Maah Daah Hey Trail. If you reach a junction with DPG Road 809 heading south, then you've passed the trail crossing. To reach *Bennett Camp* leave U.S. 85 about 7.5 miles north of Grassy Butte, or 2.0 miles south of Summit Campground, at a sign for the camp. Drive four miles west on Bennett Creek Road, then turn south onto gravel DPG Road 824 at a cattle guard. Drive south, then west to reach the camp in another two miles. To reach the crossing of the Maah Daah Hey Trail and DPG Road 823, bear right at the cattle guard, and continue on the gravel road for another four miles.

Distance: 21.8 miles one way.
Maps: DPG Maah Daah Hey Trail Map; Trails Illustrated Theodore Roosevelt National Park (#259); USGS Squaretop Butte, Wolf Coulee, and Buckskin Butte, ND 7.5-minute quadrangles; and Map D, *page 52.*

This long stretch of the Maah Daah Hey Trail illustrates how isolated the North Dakota badlands can be. In 22 miles the trail crosses only one lonely paved road that probably sees a few vehicles a day, at most. But where people are rare, wildlife is more common. This is a good trail to take if you're after sightings of mule deer, pronghorn antelope, or migrating birds. As an added bonus, there are two options for loop trips on this section. The completion of the new Bennett and Cottonwood trails has made a 15.4-mile loop all on single track at the north end of this section. A 22-mile loop that combines 10 miles of Maah Daah Hey Trail, 1.5 miles of the Ice Caves Trail plus 10 miles of little-traveled DPG Road 808 and DPG Road 809 would provide some easier riding.

One of the joys of the Maah Daah Hey Trail is the diversity of terrain. The easiest walking is on the high flat grasslands where the views stretch to the horizon and the wildlife watching is the best. The few creeks that

Maah Daah Hey Trail at MP-65

drain this arid land offer shelter, food, and water for wildlife. But the most visually stunning areas are the badlands, where the forces of falling water have sculpted a wild and unique terrain. Between County Road 50 and Bennett Creek, the Maah Daah Hey Trail explores all three of these ecosystems. Should you have time to visit only part of the trail, this section will show you what the trail is about, and will lure you back to explore its entire length.

From the junction with the *Magpie Trail* at 58.2 miles, the Maah Daah Hey Trail heads east to a normally easy crossing of signed Magpie Creek. In spring, the combination of a modest water flow and a flat shaded meadow on the north bank make this an excellent camping spot. On the north side of the creek, cross an old two-track road, which connects an old corral on the left with an old ranch building on the right.

Beyond the creek, crest a gentle hill and pass a small pond nestled in a shaded grove on the left. Pass MP 59 before crossing through a self-closing gate and dropping into a deep, dry wash lined with cotton-woods. The trail crosses another old two-track road before reaching a flowing well, stock tank, and weed-covered pond next to a corral. Keep right of a fence line until the trail crosses the fence at a self-closing gate at MP 60. Then loop around the pond to a second gate.

After crossing a dry gulch, pass a small butte where fragments of pet-rified wood and lignite are eroding from a layer of bentonite. Pass MP 61 and a self-closing gate before reaching the confluence of two small washes where you may find water in shallow puddles. As the trail begins to climb, reach the junction with the *Ice Caves Trail* at 61.4 miles. The Ice Caves Trail leads 1.5 miles east to the caves, and to the Ice Caves Trailhead, located off DPG Road 808. The 0.3-mile *Aspen Trail* forms a short loop with the Ice Caves Trail near the caves.

From the Ice Caves Trail junction, the Maah Daah Hey Trail then passes to the west of Butte 2,556'. Notice how the hard caprock on top of the butte protects it from erosion and allows it to remain standing high above the surrounding landscape. North of MP 62, pass a small arch along the trail.

After crossing a small gully reach MP 63. In another 100 yards, cross a gate that marks the McKenzie-Billings county line. Cross one more coulee, which may be home to a skittish mule deer, and enjoy some flat, easy walking. Follow the level ridge top north past MP 64. Leave the ridge at a north-facing notch and pass MP 65 as you descend toward a small pond opposite a bread loaf–shaped butte. Cross a dry tributary of Beicegel Creek at a self-closing gate. You'll catch a glimpse of gravel DPG Road 809 to the west as you climb to a small divide capped with a concrete tank that will most likely be dry.

Cross little-traveled gravel DPG Road 809 at 67.5 miles. Just north of the road is a stock pond rimmed with cottonwoods that could provide an emergency supply of water. But Beicegel Creek is just beyond, and in spring there is often a modest water flow. The creek bottom is lined with lignite bands, and exposed stumps of fossilized trees are strewn about. MP 68 is on the north bank of the creek, and a nearby grove of cotton-woods would provide a nice campsite.

North of Beicegel Creek is a long hike across a gumbo-covered flat that could be hellishly sticky walking in wet weather. On the far end of the flat is a dry stock tank by the trail, and a stock pond off to the right. Look for more fragments of petrified wood on the climb away from the flat. Soon after reaching a high grassy tableland, pass MP 70 near the highpoint. Watch for the fleet, bounding forms of pronghorn here.

The pronghorn, commonly called antelope, is a uniquely American animal; the species has no close relatives. Both males and females have horns, but those of the female are shorter and are rarely pronged. If you can get close enough, you can also distinguish the males by black patches on the lower jaw, and by a black mask extending back from the nose. Pronghorns are North America's speed kings. They've been clocked at 60 miles per hour and can sustain speeds of 30–40 mph. Pronghorn are one of the state's most popular game animals. North Dakota's Game and Fish Department estimates the population at around 12,000 animals.

Leave the tableland at the head of a birch-filled draw. Down the draw is a pretty pond with relatively clean water and inviting camping. Canada geese also appreciate this site. Cross DPG Road 809 at 71.8 miles. Reach a self-closing gate near MP 72 and enter a section of state land where travelers need to stay on the trail for the next 1.5 miles.

Cross paved McKenzie County Road 50 (DPG Road 7) at 72.5 miles.

Self-supported hiking parties will find County Road 50 one of the easiest resupply points along the Maah Daah Hey Trail. The road is paved, well-signed, and the trail crossing is relatively close to U.S. 85. If you're backpacking the long stretch between Magpie and Bennett Camps, try caching water along County Road 50 and camping at one of the ponds in the valley of Beicegel Creek.

From County Road 50, hike north up and over a small ridge crest. After passing MP 73, descend into a narrow draw where a piped spring supplying a stock tank may provide water. The grove of cottonwoods below the tank makes a fine resting spot. Continue north along the narrow valley until you leave the state land and begin a switched back climb. MP 74 marks the rim of a broad tableland. A small aspen grove on the west edge of the table hides a small, partly filled pond.

Reach the intersection with the new *Cottonwood Trail* at MP 75. This trail was built in 2005 and leads north 7.1 miles to the Bennett Trail, just one-quarter mile west of Bennett Camp. On the Maah Daah Hey you'll pass one more stock tank while following the narrow extension of the tableland to the north. To the east is Cottonwood Creek. Enjoy some good creek views before dropping off the north end of the tableland near MP 76. Pass another stock tank before crossing the usually dry west fork of Cottonwood Creek at 76.5 miles. The Maah Daah Hey Trail then follows the west bank of the creek and across a number of small coulees.

Cross through a self-closing gate, which may mark the upper limit of water in Cottonwood Creek. On the next small divide is a petrified wood locality, which also offers some broader vistas. Next pass another small pond and MP 78 before detouring up a long side coulee to avoid crossing a very deep canyon. The trail continues north along Cottonwood Creek. Then the terrain turns monotonously flat and is covered in dense sagebrush. Just before leaving Cottonwood Creek to the west near the confluence with Bennett Creek and another petrified wood locality, reach the junction with the *Bennett Trail* near MP 80. This side trail leads three miles east along the south side of Bennett Creek to Bennett Camp and DPG Road 824. It is marked with a bighorn sheep head symbol on posts similar to those used for the Maah Daah Hey Trail.

Bennett Camp
to CCC Campground

McKenzie Ranger District and TRNP North Unit

Description: After climbing the spectacular China Wall, this section combines Collar Draw and Corral Creek with high grasslands along Long X Divide. The two miles of this trail in the North Unit of Theodore Roosevelt National Park are closed to mountain bikes.

General Location: Four miles south of the North Unit of Theodore Roosevelt National Park.

Highlight: The China Wall, views from Long X Divide, and the chance to see bison at Corral Creek.

Access: To reach *Bennett Camp*, leave U.S. 85 about 7.5 miles north of Grassy Butte, or two miles south of Summit Campground at a sign for the camp. Drive four miles west on Bennett Creek Road, then turn south onto gravel DPG Road 824 at a cattle guard. Drive south, then west to reach the camp in another 2.0 miles. To reach the crossing of the Maah Daah Hey Trail and DPG Road 823, bear right at the cattle guard and continue on the gravel road for another 4.0 miles. DPG Road 862 to the *CCC Campground* leaves U.S. 85 0.9 mile south of the entry to the North Unit of Theodore Roosevelt National Park, on the south side of the Little Missouri River. At 0.8 mile from the highway, keep right. At 1.3 miles turn right into the campground. The campground offers potable water, a latrine, signboard, and garbage pickup. Horses are prohibited from Loop B.

Distance: 16.0 miles one way.

Maps: DPG Maah Daah Hey Trail Map; Trails Illustrated Theodore Roosevelt National Park (#259); USGS Wolf Coulee, Sperati Point, and Long X Divide, ND 7.5-minute quadrangles; and Map D, *page 52.*

The northern section of the Maah Daah Hey Trail is one of its more unusual. This section sees much more use by horses taking advantage of the Dakota Prairie Grasslands CCC Campground and the *Summit* and *Long X trails*. However, mountain bikers are presented with a logistical problem in this section: bikers are prohibited by wilderness regulations from riding on the trail in the North Unit of Theodore Roosevelt National Park. Bikers can leave the trail north of MP 82 on DPG Road 823 and rejoin it at MP 91 on DPG 825. This is also one of the few sections where the trail follows preexisting two-track roads.

However, this is also one of the trail's most scenic sections. It starts with a ride alongside, then up and over the China Wall, a badlands formation that for many is the highlight of their trip. Hikers and horse riders will enjoy their brief brush with designated wilderness in TRNP's North Unit.

Beyond MP 80, and the intersection with the *Bennett Trail*, reach a small stock tank and a nearly weed-filled pond as you turn west up a side coulee. The north side of this coulee is called the China Wall. This imposing climb begins near MP 81 and follows a steep badlands divide toward Bennett Creek. The wall is mix of cream and terra cotta towers and turrets. The soft rock here is so vulnerable to erosion that the wall may look different every time you visit. Be prepared: the descent is every bit as steep as the climb. On the sagebrush flats north of the wall, pass MP 82 just before a signed crossing of Bennett Creek. The land north of China Wall is part of an oil patch. Reach gravel DPG Road 823 just west of a crossing with a road to a production well at 82.3 miles.

From DPG Road 823 the Maah Daah Hey Trail climbs along the edge of a gravel road. The trail makes a sharp turn to the west and switches back to climb to a long, narrow tableland where it parallels a two-track dirt road to the north. Drop off the west side of the tableland near MP 84 where the trail leaves the road and heads north along Collar Draw.

Pass a small pond at 84.8 miles with a flat area beyond it that provides some pretty camping spots. Beyond the pond, the Maah Daah Hey Trail follows the remains of a well-worn two-track road. Pass a stock tank before reaching perhaps the most remarkable fossil site along the entire trail. Here a five-foot-tall stump of fossil wood lies on its side. The

Trailpost with Maah Daah Hey symbol and "Teddy Head"

stump is attached to a five-foot-diameter circular root system that makes the fossil resemble a huge, white mushroom turned to stone.

The fossil wood found in Theodore Roosevelt National Park and the surrounding Dakota Prairie Grasslands is most often found at the base of the Sentinel Butte Formation. Scientists believe that the trees were conifers, similar to modern sequoias. Some specimens are huge, with diameters approaching eight feet. Since the root systems of the trees are typically poorly preserved, the trees probably grew in a swampy environment, similar to cypress groves of today. Visitors are allowed to collect fossil wood in the DPG, but not in the national park.

MP 86 and a six-foot-high bison fence mark the boundary of the North Unit of Theodore Roosevelt National Park. Since this part of the park has been designated a wilderness area, mountain bikes are not allowed here. Unfortunately, there is not a contiguous zone of public land between MP 86 and the point where the trail exits the North Unit, so there is yet no approved bypass trail around the park. However, the DPG and the Maah Daah Hey Trail Association hope to acquire a right-of-way through private land for the trail. Check with the DPG before planning a ride around the North Unit. From the park fence, the Little Missouri River, a guaranteed source of water, is just a mile to the west. The park section of the trail is marked by the same large posts that mark other TRNP trails.

The trail along Corral Creek explores a flat valley bottom crowded with giant sagebrush. However, there are nice views to the north of the buttes capping the Achenbach Hills, and there is always a chance of sighting one of the bison that frequent the creek bottom.

The Maah Daah Hey Trail leaves the park at MP 88 at a gate through the bison fence. Continue up the valley of Corral Creek on the south side until the valley begins to narrow. Make the crossing of the banks of Corral Creek and continue over land to a small bridge over Sawmill Gulch, then follow the switchbacks south, climbing toward Long X Divide. The trail from MP 88–90 was reconstructed in 2003 to lessen grades and ease the creek crossing. Keep climbing past MP 89 before reaching the level grasslands on Long X Divide near another stock tank. Near MP 90 the trail crosses a fence and heads due east along the section line. You'll pass two more gates and a stock tank on the right before coming to the intersection with the west end of the 5.8-mile *Long X Trail* and DPG Road 825 at 91.0 miles. Mountain bikers taking an unofficial bypass route such as the one I describe below, *see p. 84,* around the North Unit of TRNP rejoin the Maah Daah Hey at this point. The Long X Trail turns left along the dirt road and is marked with posts branded with a large X. It provides an alternate route to the CCC Campground. Just beyond MP 91 the trail crosses another gate and another two-track road. The small grove of trees east of MP 91 provides the only shade on this open tableland.

The trail soon parallels the two-track road and follows it to the northeast across the sunny tableland. After entering state lands the trail moves west of the two-track road briefly, rejoins it, then passes a stock tank. Beyond MP 92 a stock tank and pond lie on opposite sides of the trail. As the trail reaches the end of the tableland, views to the north stretch into the national park and include the North Unit Visitor Center. Leave the state lands after MP 93, and soon after begin the descent off the tableland down switchbacks at a self-closing gate. At the base of the tableland at 93.5 miles is the intersection with the 3.8-mile *Summit Trail,* which leads east to the DPG Summit Campground off U.S. 85. The DPG plans to rebuild part of the MDH, and much of the Summit Trail, near this junction in 2006.

After MP 94, pass a modest amount of petrified wood and a small stock pond. The Maah Daah Hey Trail next climbs to a small divide with a trail sign indicating that the CCC Campground is only one-quarter mile away, the Summit Trail is two miles, and Bennett Creek is 18 miles. Here the trail splits to enter the campground from the south and west. The right fork is the 0.2-mile *CCC Trail* and drops into a steep gully before reaching the CCC Campground at 96 miles. The left fork goes over the ridge past MP 97, another stainless steel marker post, and photo opportunity.

If you have completed the Maah Daah Hey Trail, this is your holy grail. Congratulations on completing one of the longest and most unique trails in our country's system of national grasslands.

North Unit Mountain Bike Bypass Route

McKenzie Ranger District

Between mileposts 86 and 88 the Maah Daah Hey Trail passes through the North Unit of Theodore Roosevelt National Park. Besides the protection that this area receives as part of the national park, most of the North Unit is further protected as part of the Theodore Roosevelt Wilderness Area. Designation as a wilderness area means that mountain bikes, or any other mechanical vehicles, are not allowed on this section of trail. Though this designation does not affect hikers or horse riders using the trail, it creates a major problem for bikers.

One-quarter mile of the land bordering the park adjacent to the Maah Daah Hey Trail is privately owned, and there is not a continuous strip of public land available. Therefore, the Dakota Prairie Grasslands has been unable to build a bypass around the North Unit analogous to the Buffalo Gap Trail, which bypasses a wilderness area in the South Unit of TRNP. Some riders have been able to work out short-term agreements with the owner of the quarter-mile section, but it is unlikely that this will be a long-term solution for most riders. Because much of the land between Bennett Creek and Corral Creek is privately owned, a long detour over public access roads is required to regain the Maah Daah Hey where it crosses DPG Road 825 on Long X Divide near MP 91.

Three options are available to mountain bikers for getting around the North Unit. Riders can leave the Maah Daah Hey Trail on the Cottonwood Trail (MP 75), the Bennett Trail (MP 80), or on DPG Road 823 (MP 82.3). All three routes return to the Maah Daah Hey on DPG Road 825 near MP 91.

To use the Cottonwood Bypass, leave the Maah Daah Hey Trail at the intersection with the Cottonwood Trail at MP 75 and ride 7.1 miles north on Cottonwood and 0.2 mile east on the Bennett Trail to Bennett Camp. Follow the directions for the Bennett Bypass to reach the Maah Daah Hey Trail at MP 91. This bypass route is 19.8 miles long and is 3.8 miles longer than staying on the Maah Daah Hey Trail.

To use the Bennett Bypass, exit the Maah Daah Hey near MP 80 onto the Bennett Trail, and ride 3.1 miles east to the Bennett Camp Trailhead on DPG Road 824. Follow gravel DPG Road 824 2.0 miles east and north to reach the junction with DPG Road 823, which is the second bypass option. For both options ride 4.0 miles east to U.S. 85, 1.0 mile north on U.S. 85, then turn west onto DPG Road 825. Ride 5.5 miles north and west on DPG Road 825 to reach the crossing of the Maah Daah Hey Trail at MP 91 on Long X Divide. This bypass route is 15.5 miles long and is 4.5 miles longer than staying on the Maah Daah Hey.

Riders who exit the Maah Daah Hey Trail on the Bennett Trail will miss the China Wall, one of the trail's highlights. A third bypass that includes the wall, but involves less single track, is to continue on the Maah Daah Hey over the China Wall and exit at DPG Road 823 at 82.3 miles. Ride east on Road 823 to the junction with the main bypass and DPG Road 824. Then follow the directions above for the main bypass to reach the crossing of the Maah Daah Hey Trail at MP 91 on Long X Divide. This bypass route is 14.5 miles long and adds an extra 5.8 miles to the Maah Daah Hey Trail.

Dakota Prairie Grasslands

THE DAKOTA PRAIRIE GRASSLANDS is a unique mix of badlands, prairie, and grassland set in a rugged and remote region. Once home mostly to solitary cattle ranches and isolated oil wells, the grasslands has seen an explosion of interest in recreation. It has responded with a bounty of trails for those seeking experiences ranging from extended expeditions to shorter loop trips.

The Dakota Prairie Grasslands (DPG) is managed by the U.S. Department of Agriculture, Forest Service. The DPG has three units in North Dakota and one in northernmost South Dakota. The Sheyenne Ranger District covers 70,000 acres in the eastern part of the state and includes a 28-mile section of the North Country National Scenic Trail and the 7.8-mile Hankinson Hills Trail. The Grand River (155,000 acres in South Dakota) and Cedar River (6,700 acres in North Dakota) straddle the state line and include the new 6.7-mile Blacktail Trail. The bulk of the DPG is the 1 million acres of the Little Missouri National Grasslands (LMNG), which covers much of the western part of the state. The LMNG is large enough to be split into the northern McKenzie and southern Medora ranger districts.

The Forest Service manages national grasslands much like it manages national forests, except of course that there are fewer trees. These are multiple-use areas, and still heavily used for cattle ranching. The western Dakotas contain significant oil and gas fields, which are accessed by a maze of gravel roads through otherwise nearly empty country. The construction of the Maah Daah Hey Trail has jump started a new emphasis on recreation use of the grasslands, which is becoming a popular destination for hikers, mountain bikers, and horse riders.

Driving the Dakota Prairie Grasslands

To navigate the Dakota Prairie Grasslands, a grasslands map or the Maah Daah Hey Trail map is essential. Many of the roads are laid with the distinctive reddish-colored gravel known as "scoria," which is formed from clay that is burned by coal lignite fires. These roads are generally passable in wet weather. However, roads that lack gravel can be impassable when wet or even damp. Many road intersections have signs; however some do not. Also, new roads are continually under construction, and even the newest maps are not always up to date. Attention to the map, your direction of travel, and to the car odometer are critical. Motorized vehicles in the DPG are restricted to existing and marked roads, and are prohibited from trails.

The Trail System

Like national forests, the Dakota Prairie Grasslands contains recreation facilities such as campgrounds and picnic areas. However, due to the ease of travel through this open terrain, national grasslands in general have historically lacked developed trail systems. With the development of the Maah Daah Hey Trail, the DPG has perhaps the best, and largest, trail system of any grasslands in the USFS system.

The current trail system in the DPG uses the 96 miles of the Maah Daah Hey Trail as a backbone. The second longest trail on the LMNG is the Buffalo Gap Trail, a route that was built as a means for mountain bikers to get around the section of the MDH that passes through the South Unit of Theodore Roosevelt National Park. Similarly, the Long X and Summit Trails provide loop options and campground access to the north end of the MDH, and have proven especially popular with horse riders. The newest trails in the LMNG are spurs that connect the Maah Daah Hey to the overnight campgrounds along the trail.

The Dakota Prairie Grasslands has ambitious and exciting plans for expanding its trail system. Under review is a proposed 40-mile extension of the Maah Daah Hey Trail south to the Burning Coal Vein Campground, which perhaps some day could be extended even farther to White Butte, the highest point in North Dakota.

Camping and Picnic Areas

In addition to the four new camping areas constructed along the Maah Daah Hey Trail, and described in that chapter, there are five other campgrounds and one picnic area in the Dakota Prairie Grasslands. Sather Campground is located in the northwest corner of the grasslands at the junction of ND 16 and ND 68 at Sather Lake. The site has picnic tables, shelters, and vault toilets, but no hookups. By the lake, there is a fishing pier and two boat ramps.

The CCC Campground near the North Unit of Theodore Roosevelt National Park marks the northern end of the Maah Daah Hey Trail. There are 38 sites in three loops with picnic tables. There are vault toilets and potable water. In summer, the camping fee is $6 per night. This is a popular campground with horse groups.

The Summit Campground is also popular with horse parties and is found at the eastern end of the Summit Trail on DPG Road 859 off U.S. 85, just five miles south of the North Unit of Theodore Roosevelt National Park. This campground has pull-through campsites, two walk-in sites, and picnic shelters.

The Buffalo Gap Campground is located west of Medora at Exit 18 off I-94. There are 37 sites with relatively deluxe accommodations including flush toilets and coin-operated showers. The 1.3-mile Buffalo Gap Loop Trail and the 0.1-mile Buffalo Gap View Trail both begin at the campground. A 1.3-mile spur connects to the Buffalo Gap Trail. The campground is open from Memorial Day to Labor Day, and the cost is $6.00 per night.

The Burning Coal Vein Campground is located 14 miles north of Amidon on DPG Road FH3, near the Little Missouri River. This primitive campground has five sites with sheltered picnic tables and a vault toilet. The DPG hopes to extend the Maah Daah Hey Trail south to this campground. The campground name comes from a now-extinguished underground coal fire similar to that found along the Coal Vein Trail in the South Unit of Theodore Roosevelt National Park. The *Juniper Spur Trail* leads from the campground 0.3 mile to a lookout point.

Whitetail Picnic Area is located four miles west of Fairfield off U.S. 85 on Whitetail Road. There are ten picnic sites and a vault toilet. The area may be inaccessible during high water.

Buffalo Gap Trail

Medora Ranger District

Description: An exciting trail for mountain bikers that bypasses the wilderness area in the South Unit of Theodore Roosevelt National Park.
General Location: Five miles west of Medora, North Dakota.
Highlight: Fun riding single track that mixes grasslands and badlands terrain.
Access: For the *Buffalo Gap Trailhead*, take Exit 18 from I-94 west of Medora. Turn north and follow the paved road to reach the Buffalo Gap Campground in one mile. A spur trail leading to the main trail leaves from the north end of the campground. Many riders start at the Maah Daah Hey Trail *Wannagan Camp*, which can be reached from I-94 off Exit 23. Follow gravel DPG Road 730 north to the intersection with gravel DPG Road 726. Turn east on Road 726, and keep right at the intersection with Road 729. About a mile past the junction with 729, turn left onto gravel DPG Road 726-15, which is the entry road for the campground. The south end of the Buffalo Gap Trail is most easily reached from the Maah Daah Hey Trail at MP 2.3, from either the south end at Sully Creek Campground, or from the crossing of I-94 near Exit 24.
Distance: The main trail is 18.9 miles long. The spur to Buffalo Gap Campground is 1.3 miles long. Most riders completing the trail start at Wannagan Creek and ride to Medora for a 27-mile trip.
Maps: DPG Maah Daah Hey Trail Map; Trails Illustrated Theodore Roosevelt National Park (#259); USGS Wannagan Creek East, Wannagan

Creek West, Buffalo Gap Campground, and Medora, ND 7.5-minute quadrangles; and Map D, *page 52.*

The Buffalo Gap Trail was completed in 2002 to provide mountain bike riders a route around the wilderness area in the South Unit of Theodore Roosevelt National Park. Since hikers and horse riders have access to the more scenic terrain in the national park, it is likely that the trail will see far more fat tires than hoof prints or footprints. The Dakota Prairie Grasslands has done an excellent job designing this trail. Though there are few technical sections, several short pitches are steep enough to cause most riders to walk their bikes. Scenic badlands areas along Wannagan and Andrews creeks are interspersed with fast-paced riding in the trail's middle section. Most of the area is subject to grazing, but riders will also cross three prairie dog towns along the route. Expect a bit of rough riding where the trail is pockmarked from heavy cattle use.

The trail begins at a signed junction with the Maah Daah Hey Trail on the south side of a large stock dam at the 13.9-mile mark. To reach this junction from Wannagan Camp, ride 3.5 miles south on the Wannagan and Maah Daah Hey trails. The Buffalo Gap Trail is marked with large

Buffalo Gap Trail

wooden posts similar to those used on the Maah Daah Hey Trail, but branded with the image of a buffalo skull and the trail name. The DPG plans to add mileposts to Buffalo Gap in 2006. The trail is mostly single track and is generally easy to follow, except for those inevitable places where it becomes confused with cattle paths.

From the Maah Daah Hey junction, turn west and follow the south bank of a small tributary to the main stem of Wannagan Creek. Don't cross the creek, but turn south near a flowing water well at 1.5 miles, and enter a large prairie dog town. Be careful not to lose the trail amid myriad cattle paths, and watch for a broad switchback leading up to a ridge crest. The ridge provides several miles of very scenic riding along the south side of the Wannagan Creek badlands.

The trail leaves the ridge down a steep set of switchbacks to enter rolling grasslands and crosses two small drainages. Just as riding across the badlands would be nearly impossible in wet weather, this shadeless section would be unappealing riding in the full heat of summer. Cross an unnamed spur of DPG Road 730, then continue to ride west alongside gravel Road 730 before abruptly turning south and crossing it. Continue south across the grasslands, and cross another unnamed spur road. Cross one tributary of Knutson Creek before crossing the main stem near a pair of signs. Normally this crossing would be barely enough to wet your tires, but water levels could be higher during spring runoff. Beyond Knutson Creek, cross DPG Road 726, then ride alongside it to the signed junction with the Buffalo Gap Spur Trail at 10.8 miles. The junction is located immediately north of a second crossing of Road 726.

The Buffalo Gap Spur Trail leads a roundabout 1.3 miles to the campground. Facilities here include campsites, potable water, showers, kiosk, and a gazebo especially welcome to those looking to hide from the sun. The ride back to the junction with the main trail via the paved campground road and gravel DPG Road 726 is 1.8 miles, but probably just as fast as the direct route via the spur. Riders looking for more scenery, less shuttling, and a shorter trip on the Buffalo Gap Loop Trail should start at the campground and ride south into Medora. The DPG has also built the 1.3-mile, hard surface *Buffalo Gap Loop Trail*, which leads north to a small dam, and the 0.1-mile *Buffalo Gap View Trail* (a short hike to the top of a scoria knob within the campground). The Buffalo Gap Loop Trail is also open to mountain bikes and horses.

From the junction with the spur trail, the main Buffalo Gap Trail turns east and follows alongside DPG Road 726D past the Buffalo Gap Ranch. This guest ranch caters to trail users with services including lodging plus a steakhouse and bar. From the guest ranch the trail again turns south and follows a fun, fast track to a small draw where the trail crosses beneath I-94 in a wide cattle-sized culvert. Though some might find this brief trip underground a bit creepy, others will appreciate a cool break from the unrelenting sun.

Beyond I-94, the Buffalo Gap Trail swings out of sight of the interstate around a butte, and enters the badlands around Andrews Creek. Enjoy a scenic descent into the valley that holds Andrews Creek, paved Old Highway 10, and the bridge of the Burlington Northern Railroad. Riders eyeing the railroad should banish any fantasy of converting this line to a rail trail. If you've ever spent the night in Medora, you know that this is an active, hard-working railroad.

From Andrews Creek, climb to a crossing of gravel DPG Road 745 (West River Road). Enjoy a few more miles of scenic badlands riding before reaching the signed junction with the Maah Daah Hey Trail at 18.9 miles. Here the Maah Daah Hey leads either north 2.8 miles to I-94, or 2.3 miles south to Sully Creek State Park and 5.5 miles to Medora. If you need to return to Medora, the two routes will take about the same time. An unofficial mountain bike trail also leads east along the ridge top from this junction.

Other Dakota Prairie
Grasslands Trails

The 0.3-mile *Juniper Spur Trail* leads to a viewing point near the Burning Coal Vein Campground.

The *Buffalo Gap Loop Trail* is a 1.3-mile hard surface trail open to non-motorized use that starts at the DPG Buffalo Gap Campground. The 1.3-mile *Buffalo Gap Spur Trail* connects the campground to the main Buffalo Gap Trail. Adding to the confusion of similarly named trails is the 0.1-mile *Buffalo Gap View Trail*, which is located within the campground and leads to a vista on a scoria knob.

Several short trails branch off the Maah Daah Hey Trail and are described in more detail in the Maah Daah Hey Trail chapter. The *Wannagan* (0.2 mile), *Elkhorn* (0.3 mile), *Magpie* (0.3 mile), *Bennett* (3.1 miles), and *CCC* (0.2 mile) trails all lead from the Maah Daah Hey to their respective camps.

The *Ice Caves Trail* (1.5 miles) connects the Maah Daah Hey Trail and the caves to a trailhead on DPG Road 713. The *Aspen Trail* (0.3 mile) forms one side of a short loop near the middle of the Ice Caves Trail. The Ice Caves Trail can also be combined with the Maah Daah Hey Trail from the Ice Caves junction north to the crossing of DPG Road 809 for a 22-mile loop that has 12 miles of single track (the MDH and Ice Caves trails) and 10 miles of low-traffic gravel road (DPG roads 808 and 809).

Backpacker on the Maah Daah Hey Trail near Elkhorn Ranch.

The *Cottonwood Trail* was built by the DPG in 2005. This trail connects the Maah Daah Hey and Bennett trails forming a 15.4-mile loop that is sure to become popular with hikers, mountain bikers, and horse riders. The 7.1-mile trail begins at MP 75 on the Maah Daah Hey Trail and turns east to cross Cottonwood Creek. After sweeping around the head of the creek, the trail reaches the higher grasslands, which it traverses for several miles. The trail crosses three fences and two old roads before descending to end at the Bennett Trail, about one-quarter mile west of Bennett Camp.

The *Long X Trail* starts on DPG Road 825 on Long X Divide near MP 91 on the Maah Daah Hey Trail. The first half mile follows Road 825 north, then the trail becomes single track. Near the midpoint, the trail leads down to the Little Missouri River bottomlands to end at the west end of DPG CCC Campground. The trail is 5.8 miles long. The popular loop with the Maah Daah Hey Trail covers 11 miles.

The *Summit Trail* connects the DPG Summit Campground near U.S. 85 to the Maah Daah Hey Trail between MP 93 and MP 94. The 3.8-mile long trail leaves the campground heading north, follows a short stretch of DPG Road 842, then turns west to follow an unnamed draw to the Maah Daah Hey intersection. The Dakota Prairie Grasslands plans a major reconstruction of this trail. The west end of the original route follows an old cow path along a draw before climbing steeply to meet the Maah Daah Hey. The DPG plans to move the trail about one-half mile west to follow a more scenic ridge crest. This trail is most popular with horse groups using the campground and trailhead parking at the Summit Campground.

North Country
National Scenic Trail

Somewhat out of the range of this guidebook is the North Dakota segment of the North Country National Scenic Trail (NCNST). However, the existing North Country Trail is the second longest in the grasslands and easily warrants stretching some boundaries. Like the more famous Appalachian and Pacific Crest national scenic trails, the North Country Trail has been designated by Congress, is administered by the National Park Service, and is designed to provide national caliber recreation opportunities. The North Country Trail is envisioned as a 4,000-mile trail leading through seven states from Lake Champlain near Crown Point State Historic Site in New York to Lake Sakakawea State Park near the Garrison Dam on the Missouri River in North Dakota. Here the North Country Trail ends where it joins the route of the Lewis and Clark National Historic Trail. The North Country Trail was conceived in the 1970s. Trail construction has been steady, but slow, since then. As of 2005, 1,700 trail miles have been built and certified. One obstacle for the trail builders and designers is the lack of public lands for the trail corridor across much of the proposed route. This problem is especially acute across eastern and central North Dakota where there is very little public land.

Sheyenne National Grasslands Section

Luckily for North Dakotans, there is a 28-mile section of the trail in place in the Sheyenne National Grassland, just east of Lisbon in the southeast corner of the state. The trail wanders through grasslands far more heavily used by cattle than humans. The trail was resurfaced with compact gravel between the east and west trailhead in 2005, and it is marked by the DPG's branded wooden posts. Trail users will find both artesian wells (with a high concentration of dissolved minerals) and windmill-powered wells (summer only) that deliver nonpotable water for cattle. The DPG also installed self-closing gates across the cattle fences in 2005.

Motorized vehicles are not allowed on the trail, but the trail is open to horses and mountain bikes. Leave No Trace camping is permitted anywhere on the grasslands, except at trailheads. Due to the lack of firewood, camp stoves are essential. Hunting (white-tail deer and turkey) and fishing are also popular uses of this area.

The original route of the North Country Trail has been replaced with a new route by the Dakota Prairie Grasslands. From the East Trailhead on County Road 23 the trail crosses the county road at 0.4 mile. The next section is perhaps the best short hike for those who have the time for only a sample of the trail. There is a potential campsite with shade and nearby water where a bridge crosses Iron Spring Creek at 4.2 miles. This area can be wet in spring and is an excellent place for bird watching. The trail next crosses several grasslands roads before turning south away from the Sheyenne River and reaching County Road 53 at 13.2 miles. The trail crosses the Canadian Pacific Railroad line at 19.0 miles and ND 27 at 22.1 miles. From ND 27 the trail continues southwest to reach the West Trailhead on County Road 54 at 28.2 miles.

The East Trailhead is located on Richland County Road 23, seven miles north of the junction with ND 27. A short, dead-end section of the old trail extends east from the East Trailhead. The DPG is considering building a new campground at the East Trailhead. The West Trailhead is located on Ransom County Road 54, south of the crossing of ND 27.

Fort Ransom State Park Section

A 1.9-mile section of the North Country Trail is located about 20 miles northwest of the Sheyenne National Grassland section in Fort Ransom State Park. This 890-acre park was opened in 1979. Here the North Country Trail follows the west bank of the Sheyenne River across the length of the park. This trail segment is also open to mountain biking, horseback riding, cross-country skiing, and snowshoeing. There are seven other trails in the park, covering 7.1 miles, including one segment of the Sheyenne Valley Snowmobile Trail. Except for the 0.3-mile Riverside Trail, horses and mountain bikes are allowed on the trails in Fort Ransom.

The park is located about two miles north of the town of Fort Ransom on the Sheyenne River on the Walt Hjelle Parkway. The park is a fee area.

Lake Sakakawea State Park Section

The western end of the North Country National Scenic Trail is also complete. The trail ends at Lake Sakakawea State Park, near Pick City, North Dakota, and the Garrison Dam. The final 1.8 miles of the North

Country Trail lead along the shore of Lake Sakakawea south to ND 200. In the park, the North Country Trail intersects the 2.9-mile Shoreline Trail, the 0.4-mile Overlook Trail, and the 0.2-mile Whitetail Trail.

The park is located two miles north of Pick City off ND 200. It has a full-service marina, cabins, campgrounds, a store, and a swimming beach. There are also public campgrounds operated by the Army Corps of Engineers near Garrison Dam.

Blacktail Trail

The Blacktail Trail is a 6.7-mile loop trail in the Grand River National Grassland near the Shadehill Reservoir south of Lemmon, South Dakota. The loop was built in 2004 and is open to hikers, mountain bikes, and horses. It has a hardened surface and is marked by the familiar DPG branded posts.

From the junction of U.S. 12 and South Dakota 73, just west of Lemmon, South Dakota, drive about 15.5 miles south on SD 73 past the Llewellyn Johns State Recreation Area and across the Grand River. Turn east onto the access at the Pasture 9 Wildlife Area to reach the trailhead. The Dakota Prairie Grasslands plans new work on this trailhead, which will have parking, signs, toilets, and covered picnic tables. The DPG plans to add mileposts to this trail in 2006.

The trail leads north along the outlet stream below Pasture 9 Dam. It heads north across an old road, then crosses a small stock dam, and winds around the north end of a small butte. On the south end of the loop the second of two self-closing gates marks the approach to the Pasture 9 Dam.

Adjacent to the Blacktail Trail is the Shadehill Reservoir and South Dakota's Shadehill Recreation Area. The recreation area has 52 campsites with showers and electric hookups, four picnic areas, three cabins, and a lodge. Recreation facilities include a swimming area (always a welcome sight after a sweaty hike) and three boat ramps. The recreation area charges a fee, and reservations can be made for the overnight facilities. On the south side of the lake is the Hugh Glass Lakeside Use Area, which has 13 primitive campsites for horse campers that are offered on a first-come, first-served basis. There are no other designated trails in the recreation area, but the combined state park and national grasslands offer nearly 6,000 acres for riding.

A second South Dakota State Park, the Llewellyn Johns Recreation Area is located on the Shadehill entrance road closer to SD 73. The park is adjacent to Flat Creek Lake and has ten campsites with electrical hookups, but no showers.

The Shadehill Dam was built by the U.S. Bureau of Reclamation in 1951. The 145-foot-high earthen dam backs up the Grand River to create a 5,000-acre lake. The dam does not generate power.

Hankinson Hills Trail

The Hankinson Hills are four square miles of wooded sand hills between the towns of Hankinson and Mantador in the southeast corner of North Dakota. This outlying area of the Sheyenne National Grassland contains the 7.8-mile Hankinson Hills Trail. This trail was built in 2004 for use by hikers, mountain bikers, and horse riders. The trail has a compact gravel surface similar to the North Country Trail and is marked with sturdy wooden posts. The loop traverses a wooded sand hills terrain.

The Dakota Prairie Grasslands plans to add mileposts to this trail in 2006 and also hopes to build a campground near the trailhead. Most use of the trail is by horse groups. ATVs are not allowed on the trail, but unfortunately have been using it anyway.

MAP E: White Butte Route

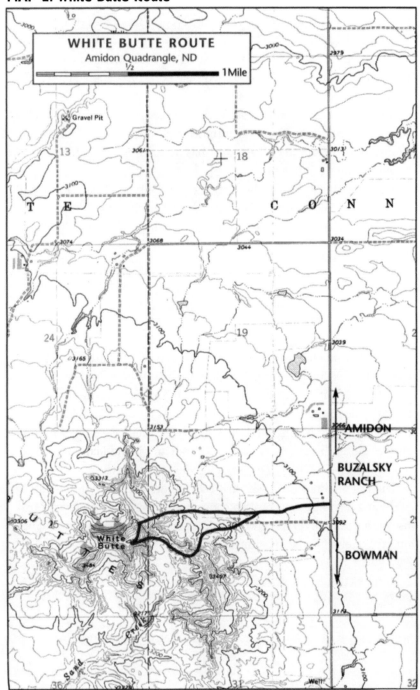

WHITE BUTTE ROUTE
Amidon Quadrangle, ND
½
1 Mile

Other
North Dakota Areas

White Butte Route

Highest Point in North Dakota

Description: An easy off-trail hike across private land to the highest point in North Dakota.
General Location: Seven miles south of Amidon, North Dakota.
Highlight: Surprising views and prairie scenery.
Access: From Amidon, drive east 2.0 miles on U.S. 85. Then turn south and drive 6.5 miles on a gravel road to the Dennis Ranch. Stop at the ranch and ask permission to make the climb. White Butte is directly west.
Distance: About three miles round trip.
Maps: USGS Amidon, ND 7.5-minute quadrangle and Map E, *page 100.*

The highest point in North Dakota lies in the Chalky Buttes in the southwest part of the state. The buttes form a major divide between the Little Missouri River on the west, and Cedar Creek and the Cannonball River, which drain east into the Missouri River. White Butte can be easily climbed in half a day, and it is close to U.S. 85, the road that connects the Black Hills to Theodore Roosevelt National Park. The trip is especially popular with "highpointers," those who aspire to climb the high points of all fifty states.

The Chalky Buttes are exceptionally pretty. To the south of White Butte, at the head of Sand Creek, are badlands that equal some of those found in Theodore Roosevelt National Park, or the Sage Creek Wilderness in South Dakota's Badlands National Park. To the west, across U.S. 85, are the Dakota Prairie Grasslands and the Black Buttes.

There are no trails or established routes up White Butte. Hike west from the gravel road about one-half mile across a field. From the field, the route to the summit is straightforward. Either climb due west to the top, or swing south and climb up the southeast ridge. There is a USGS marker, confirming that you have reached the 3,506-foot summit, and a register on top. Numerous visitors have reported seeing rattlesnakes in the area.

White Butte lies on the southwest side of the Williston Basin, a major oil-producing region. In the center of the Williston Basin the bedrock is mostly Paleocene-age Sentinel Butte Formation. The Chalky Buttes are a relict island of younger Oligocene-age White River Group sedimentary rocks standing above the prairie. The tops of White Butte, Radio Tower Butte, and Black Butte are capped by even younger Tertiary sedimentary rocks.

For many years a sign on U.S. 85 caused confusion about the location of White Butte. The sign seemed to point to a butte and radio tower only a mile east of the highway. At 3,472 feet, the Radio Tower Butte is still one of the highest points in the state, but not the highest. The sign has been moved to a point east of Amidon so that it now points to the correct butte. This confusion has caused several "highpointers," and a few North Dakota natives, to return to the Chalky Buttes to reach the correct summit.

White Butte and the surrounding land are on property now owned by the Daryle and Mary Dennis family. Please respect their private property, and ask at the ranch for permission to cross their land. If no one is at the ranch, permission to cross is not mandatory. The Dennis family's phone number is 701-879-6310. The Dennis family will collect donations to keep up the property. For more information about White Butte, check the highpointers website at www.americasroof.com.

Travois–Indian Trails Loop

Little Missouri State Park

Description: A journey from the prairie to the Little Missouri River for horses and hikers.

General Location: Twenty-one miles northeast of Killdeer, North Dakota.

Highlight: Primitive horse trails in a natural setting.

Access: From Killdeer, drive 19.0 miles north on North Dakota Highway 22. Turn east onto the gravel park road and drive two miles to the trailhead, which is located by the campground.

Distance: The loop is four miles around.

Maps: Little Missouri State Park Trail Map; USGS Mandavee SW, ND 7.5-minute quadrangle; and Map F, *page 104.*

Little Missouri State Park is a hidden gem for horse riders seeking to explore the North Dakota badlands. A large network of trails is concealed in a small state park. The park is maintained for visitors seeking camping and little-developed horseback and hiking trails. The park campground now has electrical hookups, and there are corrals and artesian wells for horses. A horse riding concession, horse rentals, and guide service is available in season. The trail map for Little Missouri shows 15 miles of trails covering 47 miles. A loop combining the Travois and Indian trails is the quickest route to descend from the grassland bluffs to the Little Missouri River bottomlands 500 feet below.

Both trails leave from the north end of the campground at a gate near the northernmost horse corral. The Indian Trail leads right and descends from the bluffs through a grove of junipers, then enters badlands. Climb up a ridge, then pass a collapsed fence. Stay right at the junction with the Hogback Trail at 0.8 mile. At 1.1 miles, just before another fence, reach the junction with the Travois Trail.

MAP F: Little Missouri State Park

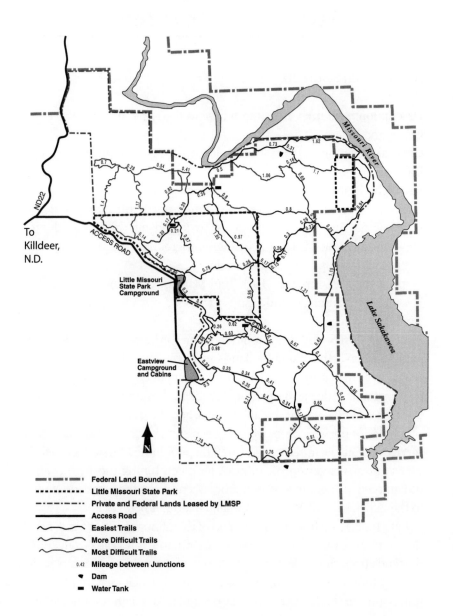

Federal Land Boundaries
Little Missouri State Park
Private and Federal Lands Leased by LMSP
Access Road
Easiest Trails
More Difficult Trails
Most Difficult Trails
0.42 Mileage between Junctions
Dam
Water Tank

104

Turn north onto the Travois Trail and descend steadily on an old road toward the Little Missouri River. The descent begins steeply through juniper, then becomes more gradual. Watch carefully for thin black lignite seams and thick bands of gray bentonite clay. The Hogback Trail intersects the Travois just before reaching the junction with the TX Trail near a stock tank at 2.1 miles. For a side trip to the river, hike due north from this intersection.

To finish the loop, turn southwest and begin to climb back toward the bluffs. The trail follows an old roadway the entire distance, but may become confused with other roads and cattle trails. You will cross one standing fence and follow a draw on the opposite side of a stock tank with a flowing well near the junction with the Cougar Canyon and Thors trails at 2.8 miles. Near the prairie rim, the Travois Trail turns abruptly southeast at another junction, before reaching the trailhead at 4.0 miles. Extending the loop on the TX Trail, which includes some riverside riding, is about eight miles.

Hikers are welcome on the trails and can often reach places inaccessible to horses. Despite the network of trails, park personnel report that there is little interest from hikers in the established trails because the terrain is so open and navigation so easy. Most groups simply follow the main canyons or ridges down to the river. Horse riders, the vast majority of park users, however, are restricted to designated trails. Trail markings are limited to short posts located at trail intersections. Corrals are available at the trailhead for those who bring their own horses.

No backcountry permits are necessary in Little Missouri State Park. Leave No Trace camping is required in the backcountry. Water can be obtained only at the trailhead campground and fires are restricted to the campground. Camping permits are $5.00 per day and $1.00 per day for horses. A ranger is stationed at the park from Memorial Day to Labor Day; otherwise self-registration is available.

Besides the solitude of a primitive park, visitors come for the wildlife watching. Coyotes, mule deer, eagles, badgers, and prairie dogs are found along with prairie rattlesnakes. The park offers an excellent topographic-based trail map. Distances between all trail junctions are shown and all trails are color-coded as easy, moderate, or difficult.

The park feels much bigger than it really is. In addition to the 4,700 acres of park land, the state leases river bottomland, which is controlled by the Army Corps of Engineers, and land from private owners. Since the land is leased for riding only there is no grazing of horses allowed. Visitors are asked not to disturb cattle and should avoid riding through areas where cattle are grazing.

Knife River Indian Villages National Historic Site

Knife River Indian Villages is located on the Missouri River at the confluence with the Knife River. The park visitor center is located about one-half mile north of Stanton, North Dakota, on County Road 37. The 1,578-acre park was established in 1974 and commemorates the village sites of Mandan and Hidatsa tribes that later become important trading centers after contact with white traders in the 1800s. The visitor center is open 7:30 A.M. to 4:30 P.M. mountain time (and to 6 P.M. in summer) daily except on Thanksgiving, Christmas, and New Year's Day. There is no picnic area, campground, or entrance fee. The park contains three trails (North Forest, Two Rivers, and Villages) with a total length of about 13 miles (see Map G, *page 107*).

The Mandan and Hidatsa tribes lived along the Upper Missouri River for several hundred years before their first contact with white explorers. Three subtribes of the Hidatsa—the Awatixa, the Awaxawi, and the Hidatsa-Proper—settled into prosperous villages near the confluence of the Knife and Missouri. They established permanent earthlodge villages and raised several crops, including corn, beans, squash, and sunflowers. Sakakawea was living in the villages in the winter of 1804–1805 with her French Canadian husband when they were hired to be guides and interpreters by the expedition of Lewis and Clark.

The location of the Mandan and Hidatsa on the Missouri allowed the tribes to function as middlemen for the flourishing trade between other

MAP G: Knife River Indian Villages National Historic Site

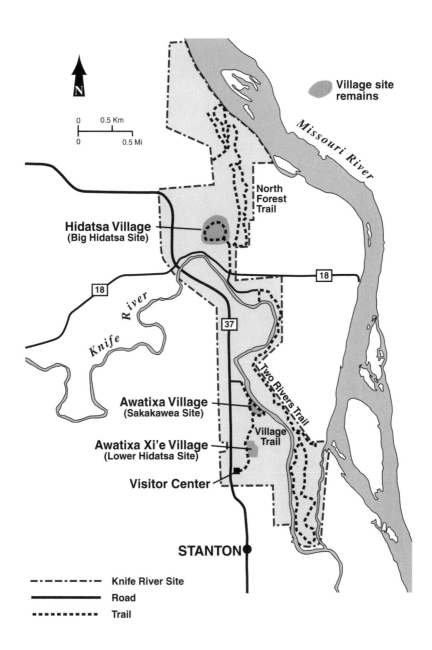

N

0   0.5 Km
0   0.5 Mi

Village site remains

Missouri River

North Forest Trail

Hidatsa Village
(Big Hidatsa Site)

18

18

Knife River

37

Two Rivers Trail

Awatixa Village
(Sakakawea Site)

Village Trail

Awatixa Xi'e Village
(Lower Hidatsa Site)

Visitor Center

STANTON

Knife River Site
Road
Trail

tribes. But further contact with whites and the arrival of fur traders changed the economy of the northern plains. The tribes became more dependent on manufactured goods, and as with so many other tribes, new diseases decimated their population. Along with the Arikaras, the Mandan and Hidatsa were moved upstream to the Fort Berthold Reservation in 1885.

The *Villages Trail* begins at the park visitor center and leads to both the Awatixa (Sakakawea) and Awatixa Xi'e (Lower Hidatsa) village sites. This is the best hike for those seeking to better understand life in the Knife River villages and for those who would like to walk for a while in the steps of Sakakawea. The round-trip distance for this gravel path is 1.3 miles. The loop at Awatixa Village includes a short walk along the Knife River. A spur trail leads north from the village 0.2 mile to another parking area off County Road 37.

The *Two Rivers Trail* begins from a parking area off County Road 18. The trail follows an old two-track and begins in a narrow strip of grass-land between the Knife River and cultivated land outside the park. A loop at the south end of the trail passes through a riverside forest of green ash, willow, box elder, and cottonwoods and offers views of both the Knife and Missouri rivers. This trail is 6.2-miles long and is groomed for cross-country skiing in winter.

The *North Forest Trail* begins from the north side of County Road 18. It follows an old two-track through river bottom forests with views of the Missouri River. Near the start of the trail, the Big Hidatsa Trail leads 0.2 mile to the Big Hidatsa Village. Beyond the village the trail splits twice into loops allowing hikers to make shorter trips. Near the end of the second loop are two spur trails. To the north the North Prairie Arm leads to the highest point in the park, views of the Missouri River, and the finest stand of native prairie in the park. This is a remnant of origi-nal prairie that has never been plowed. The arm is a mowed path marked by carsonite posts. (Carsonite is a material similar to fiberglass, the posts are flat and brown, with information applied on stickers.) The North Forest Trail is 5.0 miles long and is groomed for cross-country skiing in winter. The trail is more sheltered from wind and sun than Two Rivers, and it may offer skiers more reliable snow.

Fort Union Trading Post
National Historic Site

There are no trails at the third National Park Service unit in North Dakota. The Fort Union Trading Post National Historic Site was established in 1966 near the confluence of the Missouri and Yellowstone rivers. The fort was established in 1829 by the American Fur Company as a trading post with the Assiniboin, Crow, and Blackfoot Indian tribes. Trade relations gradually deteriorated and the fort was sold to the U.S. Army and dismantled in 1867. Since the National Park Service acquired the property in 1966, it has been excavating, reconstructing, and developing exhibits. Fort Union is located 24 miles southwest of Williston on ND 1804. The park is open daily except for New Year's Day and Christmas.

Cross Ranch State Park
and Nature Preserve

Cross Ranch State Park preserves seven miles of one of the last free-flowing and undeveloped stretches of the Missouri River. The narrow 590-acre park is one of the few opportunities on the northern Great Plains to hike in a wooded landscape. In addition to the trail system, the park features a visitor center, boat launch area, canoe and kayak rentals, log cabins for rent, and both tent and RV campgrounds. The park is located just a few miles downstream of the 1804 winter camp of the Lewis and Clark expedition.

The trail system is essentially a string of six main loops along the riverside covering 13.9 miles, plus a self-guided interpretive trail on Cross

Ranch Nature Preserve. At the north end of the park, the Levis Trail (2.2 miles) contains a single backcountry campsite with a vault toilet. The Gaines (3.3 miles) and Cottonwood (2.1 miles) trails are located on land owned by the Nature Conservancy's Cross Ranch Nature Preserve and follow a jeep track still used by researchers. The Matah Trail (2.9 miles) starts at the visitor center and forms a series of three smaller loops through the park's developed area. The innermost loop follows a self-guiding interpretive route for which brochures are available at the visitor center. The upper (2.0 miles) and lower (1.4 miles) loops of the Ma-ak-oti Trail begin from the Sanger Trailhead in the southern part of the park. There are steep unprotected stairs on these trails. The Ma-ak-oti Trail is open for snowshoeing in winter, while the other park trails are open to cross-country skiing. In 2004 the entire trail system was included in the National Recreation Trail System.

Adjacent to Cross Ranch State Park is the 6,000-acre Cross Ranch Nature Preserve, owned and operated by the Nature Conservancy, a private, nonprofit organization devoted to the preservation of ecologically sensitive lands and the habitats of threatened plants and animals. The ranch consists of three units covering 5,600 acres. The 1,800-acre north unit is on the banks of the Missouri and borders the state park. The other two units are on the hills above the river floodplain. There are no public facilities at ranch headquarters. The Nature Conservancy keeps bison on the central and south units of the ranch. The self-guided Prairie Trail (2.0 miles) crosses prairie, wooded draws, and bison pasture. Brochures can be found at the trailhead, located 0.75 mile north of the park entrance on the gravel road. This trail is not open for skiing.

Appendix A
Selected Bibliography

Froiland, Sven G. *Natural History of the Black Hills and Badlands*, The Center for Western Studies, 1990.

Hauk, Joy Keve. *Badlands, Its Life and Landscape*, Badlands Natural History Association, 1969.

McCullough, David. *Mornings on Horseback: The Story of an Extraordinary Family, a Vanished Way of Life and the Unique Child Who Became Theodore Roosevelt*, Simon and Schuster, 1982.

Melius, Michael. *True*, Tensleep Publications, 1991.

————— *Under Wing and Sky: Birds of the Badlands and Black Hills*, Tesseralt Publications, 1995.

Morris, Edmund. *Theodore Rex*, Modern Library, 2002.

Murphy, E. C., J. P. Bluemle, and B. M. Kaye. "A Roadlog Guide for the South and North Units Theodore Roosevelt National Park," Theodore Roosevelt Nature and History Association, 2005.

National Geographic Trails Illustrated. "Theodore Roosevelt National Park Map (#259)," 2002.

Raventon, Edward. *Island in the Plains*, Johnson Books, 1994.

Raventon, Edward. *Buffalo Country: A Northern Plains Narrative*, Johnson Books, 2003.

Rogers, Hiram. *Exploring the Black Hills and Badlands: A Guide for Hikers, Cross-country Skiers, and Mountain Bikers*, Johnson Books, 1999.

Roosevelt, Theodore. *Ranch Life and the Hunting Trail*, St. Martin's Press, 1985.

Scoch, H., and B. Kaye. *Theodore Roosevelt: The Story Behind the Scenery*, K.C. Publications, 1993.

Van Bruggen, Theodore. *Wildflowers, Grasses, and Other Plants of the Northern Plains and Black Hills*, Badlands Natural History Association, 1992.

Appendix B
Information Sources

Cross Ranch Nature Preserve, The Nature Conservancy, 1401 River Road, Center, ND 58530-9445, (701) 794-8741. www.nature.org

Cross Ranch State Park, 1403 River Road, Center, ND 58530, (701) 794-3731. crsp@state.nd.us

Dakota Cyclery, 1519 East Main Avenue, Bismarck, ND 58501, (701) 222-1218. www.dakotacyclery.com

Dakota Prairie Grasslands, 240 West Central Avenue, Bismarck, ND 58503, (701) 250-4443. www.fs.fed.us/r1/dakotaprairie

Fort Abraham Lincoln State Park, 4480 Fort Lincoln Road, Mandan, ND 58554, (701) 667-6340. falsp@state.nd.us

Fort Union Trading Post National Historic Site, 15550 Highway 1804, Williston, ND 58801, (701) 572-9083. ww.nps.gov/fous

Grand River Ranger District, P.O. Box 390, Lemmon, SD 57638, (605) 374-3592.

Knife River Indian Villages National Historic Site, P.O. Box 9, Stanton, ND 58571, (701) 745-3300. www.nps.gov/knri

Lake Sakakawea State Park, Box 732, Riverdale, ND 58565, (701) 487-3315. www.ndparks.com/Parks/LSSP.htm

Leave No Trace, Inc., P.O. Box 997, Boulder, CO 80306, (800) 332-4100. www.LNT.org

Lewis and Clark State Park, 4904 119th Road NW, Epping, ND 58843, (701) 859-3071. lcsp@state.nd.us

Little Missouri State Park. Contact Cross Ranch State Park.

McKenzie Ranger District, 1901 South Main Street, Watford City, ND 58854, (701) 842-2393.

Medora Ranger District, 161 21st Street W., Dickinson, ND 58601, (701) 225-5151.

National Geographic Trails Illustrated Maps, P.O. Box 4357, Evergreen, Colorado 80437-4357, (800) 962-1643. www.nationalgeographic.com/maps

North Country National Scenic Trail, 700 Rayovac Drive, Suite 100, Madison, WI 53711, (608) 441-5610. www.nps.gov/noco

North Country Trail Association, 229 E. Main Street, Lowell, MI 49331, (866) 445-3628. www.northcountrytrail.org

North Dakota State Parks and Recreation Department, 1600 E. Century Avenue, Suite 3, Bismarck, ND, 58503-0649, (701) 328-5357. www.ndparks.com

North Dakota Tourism Division, Century Center, 1600 E. Century Avenue, Suite 2, PO Box 2057, Bismarck, ND 58503-2057, (800) 435-5663 or (701) 328-2525. www.ndtourism.com

Peaceful Valley Ranch, P.O. Box 308, Medora, ND 58645, (701) 623-4568.

Shadehill Recreation Area, 19150 Summerville Road, Box 63, Shadehill, SD 57653, (605) 374-5114. www.sdgp.info

Sheyenne Ranger District, P.O. Box 946, Lisbon, ND 58054, (701) 683-4342.

Sully Creek State Park. Contact Fort Abraham Lincoln State Park, (701) 667-6340, www.ndparks.com, or North Dakota Parks and Recreation Department, 1600 E. Century Avenue, Suite 3, Bismarck, ND 58503, (701) 328-5357.

Theodore Roosevelt National Park, P.O. Box 7, Medora, ND 58645, (701) 623-4466 (South Unit). www.nps.gov/thro. The North Unit can be reached at (701) 842-2333.

Theodore Roosevelt Nature and History Association, P.O. Box 167, Medora, ND 58645, (701) 623-4884. www.nps.gov/thro/ tr_shop.htm

Additional Services in Medora

Ambulance (701) 623-4333

Billings County Sheriff (701) 623-4323

Chamber of Commerce (701) 623-4910,
medorachamber@midstate.net

Medora Police (701) 623-4333

St. Joseph's Hospital (Dickinson) (800) 300-4468, (701) 456-4000

Additional Services in Watford City

Ambulance and Hospital, 516 North Main Street,
Watford City, ND (701) 842-3000

McKenzie County Sheriff (701) 444-3654

Watford City Police (701) 444-2400

Hiram Rogers is the author of the best selling *Exploring the Black Hills and Badlands,* as well as the books *50 Hikes in Kentucky* and *Backroad Bicycling in the Blue Ridge and Smoky Mountains.* He has also written about the outdoor recreation and conservation issues for several magazines including *Backpacker* and GORP.com. He is a geologist, avid outdoorsman, and former resident of the Dakotas.